Unraveling the Mysteries of Case Study Research

Unraveling the Mysteries of Case Study Research

A GUIDE FOR BUSINESS AND MANAGEMENT STUDENTS

Marilyn L. Taylor

Arvin Gottlieb/Missouri Chair in Strategic Management, Henry W. Bloch School of Management, University of Missouri – Kansas City, USA

Mikael Søndergaard

Associate Professor, Department of Management, School of Business and Social Sciences, Tuborg Research Centre for Globalisation and Firms, Aarhus University, Denmark

Edward Elgar
PUBLISHING

Cheltenham, UK • Northampton, MA, USA

Published by
Edward Elgar Publishing Limited
The Lypiatts
15 Lansdown Road
Cheltenham
Glos GL50 2JA
UK

Edward Elgar Publishing, Inc.
William Pratt House
9 Dewey Court
Northampton
Massachusetts 01060
USA

A catalogue record for this book
is available from the British Library

Library of Congress Control Number: 2017931771

ISBN 978 1 78643 721 1 (cased)
ISBN 978 1 78643 723 5 (paperback)
ISBN 978 1 78643 722 8 (eBook)

Typeset by Servis Filmsetting Ltd, Stockport, Cheshire.
Printed in the United States. Printed on elemental chlorine free
(ECF) recycled paper containing 30% Post-Consumer Waste.

A word of thanks is always in order.

I want to thank my family, especially my husband Bob, daughter Theresa Taylor-Coates-Royal, and son Chris. Their forbearance of my absences have permitted developing the insights reflected in these chapters. And, their encouragement has lent me energy in my endeavors. In addition, there have been a host of mentors and colleagues who have been instrumental along this multi-decade journey. Mentors at Harvard Business School where I was an MBA and then doctoral student included C. Roland Christensen, L.B. ('By') Barnes Paul Lawrence, Jay Lorsch, Ray Bauer, and George Lombard as well as, later, colleague Michael E. Porter. Colleagues at HBS, then the University of Kansas and, more recently, at the University of Missouri at Kansas City, are too numerous to mention. As, indeed, are colleagues in my two main academic professional organizations, Academy of Management and North American Case Research Association. My thanks to all.

Marilyn Levere Taylor

Understanding and application for rigor and transparency in case research for my PhD project was provided in supervision by Flemming Agersnap and workshop presentations by Robert K. Yin. Understanding for dimensions of cultural differences as a paradigm was obtained by supportive conversations with Geert Hofstede, and an encouraging support from colleagues at the European University Institute. Thank you. Further experience with case research was obtained in contributions coauthored with, among others, Dorthe Døjbak Håkonsson, William Naumes, Harry Lane, Ole Ø. Madsen, Niels Noorderhaven. Thank you. Moreover, by supervising business and management students at University of Southern Denmark and University of Aarhus I gained further insights in case research methods. Thank you. On my journey in case research, my wife Ulla Søderberg and later my daughters Marie, Caroline and Anne-Louise provided a loving family context supporting this adventure. Thank you so much.

Mikael Søndergaard

Contents in brief

Full contents

Figures

Tables

Boxes

Foreword

I was delighted to be asked to write the Foreword to this book and I quickly said yes, since Marilyn Taylor was my classmate in the Doctoral Program at Harvard Business School (HBS) and Mikael Søndergaard has been a friend and colleague since we met many years ago through our involvement with the International Organizations Network (ION). Of course, I said yes without really thinking about what writing the Foreword actually meant, when it would be due, or what I would say. I read Forewords to other books as a guide and thought of numerous themes. Upon reading this book I realized that it contained advice that I wished someone had given to me when I started writing cases. I learned many of the lessons contained in this book the hard way through experience, so I will share some of my case-writing experiences and the lessons I learned to reinforce the advice that the authors provide.

I have written many cases, 80 or more, both teaching cases and research cases. Some were good and were used in schools around the world and were published in textbooks. And some were not so good and rarely used and some, after a lot of work, never saw the light of day. It was these latter cases that taught me many of the lessons you will read about in this book. Since the book is written for people who are about to start their case-writing journey, I will focus on my early experiences and lessons learned from them that I was able to carry forward in my career.

The first case I wrote was as a doctoral student in organizational behavior working as a course assistant. There was an article in a magazine or newspaper about an individual who instituted a different way to charge for fitness club memberships since many people joined but usually stopped going to the club after a short while. It caught my interest and the situation seemed to have some interesting organizational design issues. A cold call to this person worked and he agreed to meet with me and let me write a case about what he was doing. I think he agreed because he was delighted that someone from the Harvard Business School thought what he was doing was interesting and that it might be good publicity. I wrote the case and thought it was good. However, it described some problems and the entrepreneur was not happy and refused to release it.

The second case also written when I was a doctoral student was US luxury department store group Neiman Marcus. I visited the headquarters and a store in Dallas and a store in another location interviewing executives and store personnel. It went off without a hitch – released, used in a course at HBS, and published in an independent text. Executives from Neiman Marcus flew to Boston to attend a class and have dinner with some HBS faculty. The difference between my first and second case experience was that the faculty at HBS had a *relationship* with the company and the CEO (Richard Marcus, son of the founder Stanley Marcus). He understood what a case was and he was happy to let the school write it. Stanley Marcus ensured the participation of his executives and store managers. Any problems that might have arisen could have been handled because of the relationships.

My final case-writing experience as a doctoral student was in the form of a four-case series. The series formed the database for my dissertation.[1] My dissertation supervisor was Professor Paul Lawrence. It was a study comparing the management of R&D at National Institutes of Health (NIH) and Bell Telephone Laboratories. At that time, NIH was under pressure from the Department of Health, Education and Welfare and the Office of Management and Budget (OMB) to make more use of 'modern management methods'. These departments were concerned that NIH's autonomy was a factor in it spending too much money. At issue was the 'best way to manage R&D'. One school of thought was that R&D was not really possible to control, as it was a creative process requiring time and autonomy; and that, consequently, scientists using scientific criteria should do the planning and evaluation. The other school of thought believed that the best way to ensure progress was through targeted research and tight control systems.

The Director of NIH was previously a Dean of a university medical school and had collaborated with Paul Lawrence from when Paul had conducted a comparative study of university medical schools.[2] (Note: You should see a pattern emerging – *relationships*!) In addition to the relationship between the Director and Paul Lawrence, *NIH had a stake in the research and outcome*, believing that it was managing its R&D programs well and that Paul Lawrence and his doctoral researchers were independent and capable researchers.

One of the interesting and novel aspects of this project was that it was to be comparative with a private company. We had to find a comparative organization to study. We approached one and we struck out. They did not want to be involved. Even though the company could have learned some valuable management insights from Harvard researchers, they were not interested. It was an eye-opening experience for me. Paul Lawrence was an eminent scholar, a luminary in the field of organizational design and one of the developers of contingency theory. Why wouldn't they want to be included in one of his research studies? The lesson is that *organizations need to have a reason to be involved in a research project which will require time from their executives and they need to see some benefit from involvement.*

We succeeded with our next invitation. That invitation was to Bell Telephone Laboratories, which was engaged in a wide spectrum of basic, applied and development programs. Why did Bell agree to cooperate? We could only speculate but Bell also was feeling considerable political pressure from government about possibly being broken up as well as from existing and potential competitors. Both NIH and Bell shared a similar problem: each was a prestigious and successful R&D institution, staffed by talented people who believed in their organizational arrangements and management methods but were having trouble communicating about them with the federal government.

Bell agreed and gave us complete access to their people and programs. They assigned one of their executives 'Red' McKay to help us. Initially we thought 'Red' was simply a 'watchdog' but he turned out to be a very helpful gatekeeper who arranged access to executives and programs and provided insights we would not have developed without him.

Lessons

Take the advice in Chapter 4 very seriously. Gaining access to research sites, developing and maintaining relationships, graceful exit and obtaining permission to use or publish the data, findings or case are critical.

You may be a student in a program for working professionals (e.g., a part-time MBA) or a professor who has a working professional in the class. There may be an interesting situation at work that one of you would like to write a case about for the class. You may have access to all the necessary information but do you have permission to write it and release it? I have fallen into this trap and have seen colleagues fall into it a number of times. You need permission from the person who has authority over your unit of analysis and can grant permission to do the research and to release the case and data. And, while you are at it, ask whether or not it will have to be approved by the organization's lawyers.

Companies take their proprietary information very seriously and want it protected. As Acting Dean of a Business School, I had to discipline a professor for not following university rules and regulations and not getting the data released before publishing it. And don't make the mistake of thinking that disguising the case will be sufficient without a formal release.

I enjoyed the quotes throughout the book from Sherlock Holmes. One in particular resonated with me, which was Sherlock Holmes's 'Interesting cases only please' response to Watson's inquiry about his choice of a research site. This quote along with the advice in Chapter 5 that the general research strategy 'is to determine the best ways to contrast any differences as sharply as possible' brought back memories of my case research experience at NIH. I remember Paul Lawrence telling me to 'maximize differences' in order to find something useful and interesting. How did we do that? I have one final example before closing.

We wanted to know what made the difference between well-managed research programs and ones that were not as well managed. That was our research question. We asked NIH to identify a sample of high performers and low performers operating under relatively certain and uncertain technical and environmental (political) conditions that we believed were the important *contexts* for the programs. Early in the book you will learn that it is not just the project or program that should be your focus but that its context is important also.

NIH staff members compiled a list of 25 programs and these programs were rated by 21 anonymous scientists at NIH on a scale of 1 (poorest performance) to 7 (best performance). We used a decision rule of 75 percent response rate and 80 percent agreement on performance level to choose our sample of four programs that we felt would follow Sherlock Holmes's and Paul Lawrence's advice for 'interesting'. We chose four and had comparative programs (a high performer and a low performer in each type of environment – certain and uncertain). We began the research with a pilot study of one of the programs.

I will close with some final additional observations. Note that each chapter has a good summary of lessons in the form of questions and answers. In addition the appendices contain multiple helpful examples --- don't miss them! Finally, don't underestimate how much work and time are involved in writing good cases. I have found it to be worth the effort as I have learned a great deal about different organizations, industries and business models that have served me well in my teaching and consulting. Enjoy your case-writing experience. I certainly wish you success in your efforts and trust you find case research as meaningful and fruitful as I have.

Henry W. Lane
D'Amore-McKim School of Business
Northeastern University
Boston MA
January 2017

NOTES

1 This research project is reported in H.W. Lane, R.G. Beddows, and P.R. Lawrence (1981), *Managing Large Research and Development Programs*, New York: State University of New York Press.
2 See Weisbord, M.R., P.R. Lawrence, and M.P. Charns (1978), 'Three dilemmas of academic medical centers', *Journal of Applied Behavioral Science*, **14**(3), 284–304.

1

Welcome to your case research adventure!

You have embarked on an adventure – a journey that may be a:

- class project, solo or in a team;
- thesis that is the last milestone in your graduate degree program;
- dissertation that moves you toward that coveted PhD or equivalent degree;
- action research program in your company;
- research project or program that is part of the continuing expansion of your scholarly work;
- personal project in pursuit of knowledge.

Whatever the adventure you have chosen or have been assigned by a supervising professor, you are embarking on a case research process. In this book we want to share our ideas to help create a roadmap for your adventure. We will share our insights and experiences, as well as those of our students, colleagues and friends, and other authors we have never met.

What does the roadmap contained in this book consist of? Chapters 2 through 6 contain the 'meat' of our discussion. In this current chapter we simply want to welcome you and respond to two questions: (1) What is a case? (2) What can you expect from the chapters to follow?

1.1 What is a case?

There are multiple definitions of a case, as Box 1.1 suggests.[1] Indeed, after examining definitions used by various authors, one case research colleague suggested that it appeared that 'anything goes' (Grünbaum, 2007, p. 2) and according to another, establishing a definition is a 'morass' (Gerring, 2004, p. 342). However, as the examples in this volume demonstrate, there *is* a commonality. Case research involves gathering and describing not only the phenomenon that is of interest but also its context. Generally

---

BOX 1.1

DEFINITIONS OF A CASE STUDY OR CASE RESEARCH

'We define it as a multifaceted examination of a situation' (Christensen and Carlile, 2009, p. 243).

'Case studies are rich empirical descriptions of particular instances of a phenomenon that are based on a variety of data sources' (Eisenhardt and Graebner, 2007, p. 25, citing Yin, 1994).

'A case study is an empirical inquiry that investigates a contemporary phenomenon within a real-life context where the boundaries between phenomenon and context are not clearly evident, and in which multiple sources of evidence are used' (Yin, 1984, p. 23).

'Case studies typically combine data collection methods such as archival searches, interviews, questionnaires, and observation' (Eisenhardt, 1989, p. 534).

'While quantitative data often appears in case studies, qualitative data usually predominates' (Patton and Appelbaum, 2003, p. 60).

'In general terms, a case study is a description of a management situation. As such, it is the marketing analogue of a physician's clinical examination (e.g., McLeod, 1979) and relies on a similar appeal to multiple data sources for reliable diagnosis (cf., Leenders and Erskine, 1978)' (Bonoma, 1985, p. 203).

'Case study is the examination of an instance in action. The choice of the word "instance" is significant in this definition, because it implies a goal of generalization' (MacDonald & Walker, 1975, p. 2 as quoted in *Simons, 1996, n.p.*).

'Case research. . .can be defined as a research method that involves investigating one or a small number of social entities or situations about which data are collected using multiple sources of data and developing a holistic description through an iterative research process' (Easton, 2010, p. 119, as quoted in Dubois and Gibbert, 2010, n.p.).

'The case study is a research strategy which focuses on understanding the dynamics present within single settings' (Eisenhardt, 1989, p. 534).

---

the data will be predominantly of a qualitative nature – that is, a narrative describing the unit of analysis (see Chapter 2) *and* its setting. In some instances, however, the case data may include quantitative data. Because a case study includes content and its setting, case study research necessarily involves smaller samples. Some authors suggest upper limits on the number of cases to include in a research project before it is *not* case research. A classic article by Eisenhardt (1989) suggests a minimum of four and an upper limit of 10. Eisenhardt argues for the lower limit in order to develop more robust findings and an upper limit of 10 because of the complexity of managing and analyzing the data. However, there is no strict limit on the upper limit of the number of cases before a study is considered *not* case research.

1.2   What can you expect from the chapters to follow?

In Chapter 2 we will ask you about your personal motivation for undertaking the adventure of the case research project or program you have initiated. Once you fully confront why you are undertaking the challenge and what you want to invest in it, you can move forward to think about the research itself. The rest of Chapter 2 examines the objective of the research and the research questions that you want to ask. You will find that these two aspects are often twin mirrors, with the objective or objectives laid out in the form of questions. Those questions will help guide your research plan. Finally, we ask you to think about the unit of analysis, the entity that you are going to study – social system, a city, or, more likely in business management, an organization, a unit within an organization, or individuals – leaders or followers. Whatever the unit of analysis, above all we will remind you that case research is distinguished by its drive to understand the unit of analysis *and* its context. If the unit of analysis is a business, the industry is the important context. If it is a department, the organization is critical. If an individual or a particular role within an organization is your chosen focus, the organization and perhaps the individual's personal social system are important to understand. Case research is, after all, about developing a deeper understanding of your unit of analysis *within* its context and from the perspective of the players in the phenomenon that is your focus.

In Chapter 3 we focus on research design. In terms of design, the basic questions we will ask are whether you want to study one unit of analysis or multiple and whether you want to study that/those unit/s of analysis at a point in time or longitudinally, meaning over time. The choice you make is related to multiple factors, including the amount of time and resources you have to invest in the research (more units or a larger sample take up more of both) and what the state of the literature is. What is currently known about the phenomenon that you are about to study impacts on whether you want to generate theory because little is known, or whether you want to be at the other end of the continuum – that is, testing existing theory. Usually case research relies on multiple sources of data, but the chapter does ask, which is better – qualitative or quantitative data? Relying more heavily on qualitative or quantitative data may be a personal choice, but case research generally focuses more, as noted above, on qualitative data. Further, the differences and relationships among descriptive, predictive, and prescriptive theory are related to the answer. Box 3.2 in Chapter 3 will give you insights into the relationships among the various issues we cover.

In Chapter 4 we ask you to consider whether you want to pursue your case study by gathering primary or secondary data. Frankly, we think gathering primary data is more fun – but each can be used and case research usually uses both. Primary data – usually in the form of interviews, participant observation, and internal documents – in our personal opinion is more meaningful in many ways, especially in developing insights into the perspectives of the players in the phenomenon. But, gathering such data is also a more complex process to manage. Not only do you have to identify sites, you also have to figure out how to get entry, maintain relationships, and, finally, exit – gracefully. That, by the way, also means getting, or retaining, permission to utilize your data for your report or publication – depending on what your aim is. While you are working with your sites or subjects, you are likely to be interviewing, observing, or gathering documentation. There are special challenges involved with each – the chapter suggests what to look for. In particular, you might want to debate the pros and cons of anthropologist Clifford J. Geertz's involvement with a Balinese cockfight as part of his 'participant observation' (Geertz, 1973) and ask what you might have done under similar circumstances!

Chapter 5 assumes you have your data at least partially collected and that you are asking yourself, as Søndergaard, one of the authors of this book, did with his dissertation data: What do I do to make all this data 'talk'? Chapter 5 draws especially on the insights of Robert K. Yin (1989, 2009) who has given extensive guidance to many of us about analyzing extensive databases of qualitative data. The chapter also introduces you to content analysis, either by hand as author Taylor did with a large body of data or with the help of qualitative data analyses (QDAs) software. QDAs are not disease states. Rather, they are computer data (analysis) *assists*. QDAs do not yield analyses by themselves. But, we explain that in Chapter 5.

In Chapter 6 we ask how descriptive, predictive, and prescriptive theory are related to case research. Chapter 6 also introduces you to abductive reasoning as the consummate interlink between the inductive and deductive reasoning processes we overviewed in Chapter 3. We explain that an interpretivist approach uses both – that's right you don't have to choose! Inductive and

Figure 1.1 The rational approach to case research: hierarchical relationships among the issues

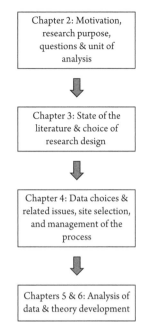

deductive thinking are *both* important in an interpretivist's world. Especially if you identify with ethnographers (we visit that research approach in Chapter 4), the interpretivist mode may be your preferred approach to understanding your body of data.

Figures 1.1 and 1.2 summarize Chapters 2 through 6. You will note that Figure 1.1 suggests a step-by-step progression through the chapters. However, in reality, the process is very iterative as Figure 1.2 suggests. Throughout Chapters 2 through 6 we provide examples of these various aspects of the process and related issues from our own experience and that of other researchers. You will also find the references for our citations at the conclusion of each chapter along with a few selected other readings that may be helpful to you as you pursue your case research journey.

Chapter 7 reflects on our case research journey in this volume and provides a summary of our set of prescriptions – the top 18 capsules of 'what you need to remember most' to make sure that your case research journey is. . .well, it may never be as smooth as you hoped, but our aim is to help you find it very satisfying. We want you to complete that class project, thesis, dissertation, action research, consulting project, or additional research project with a 'well done' from those to whom you report your process and results. And we also want you to achieve a deep sense of satisfaction in the feedback from your

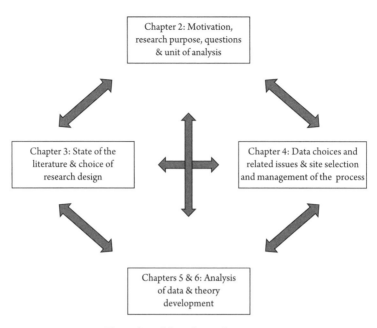

Figure 1.2 The reality of the relationships

subjects or sites that let you know that you have indeed understood them and their situation.

Along our journey we are joined periodically by the consummate case researcher and analyst himself – none other than the great Sherlock Holmes. Please enjoy his pithy remarks and think deeply about how they are related to the material in the chapter. We did, and we had fun doing so. We hope you do too!

NOTE

1 'Case studies are easier to plan than experiments, but harder to interpret and difficult to generalize' (Kitchenham, Pitchard, and Fleeger, 1995, p. 53). 'The process of building theory from case study research is a strikingly iterative one. While an investigator may focus on one part of the process at one time, the process itself involves constant iteration backward and forward between steps' (Eisenhardt, 1989, p. 546). '[T]here is no ideal number of cases, a number between 4 and 10 usually works well. With fewer than 4 cases, it is often difficult to generalize with much complexity, and its empirical grounding is unlikely to be unconvincing, unless there are several mini-cases within it. . . With more than 10 cases it becomes difficult to cope with the complexity and volume of the data' (ibid.).

REFERENCES

Bonoma, T.V. (1985), 'Case research in marketing: Opportunities problems, and a process', *Journal of Marketing Research*, **22**(2), 199–208.

Christensen, C.L. and P.R. Carlile (2009), 'Course research: Using case method to build and teach management theory', *Academy of Management Learning & Education*, **8**(2), 240–51.

Easton, G. (2010), 'Case study research: A critical realist approach', *Industrial Marketing Management*, **39**(1), 118–28.

Dubois, A. and M. Gibbert (2010), 'From complexity to transparency: Managing the interplay between theory, method and empirical phenomena in IMM case studies', *Industrial Marketing Management*, **39**(1), 129–36.

Eisenhardt, K.M. (1989), 'Building theories from case study research', *The Academy of Management Review*, **14**(4), 532–50.

Eisenhardt, K.M. and M.E. Graebner (2007), 'Theory building from cases: Opportunities and challenges', *Academy of Management Journal*, **50**(1), 25–32.

Geertz, C. (1973), 'Thick description: Toward an interpretive theory of culture', in *The Interpretation of Cultures*, New York: Basic Books, pp. 3–30.

Gerring, J. (2004), 'What is a case study and what is it good for?' *The American Political Science Review*, **98**(2), 341–54.

Grünbaum, N.N. (2007), 'Identification of ambiguity in the case study research typology: So what is a unit of analysis?' *Qualitative Market Research*, **10**(1), 78–97.

Kitchenham, B., L. Pitchard, and S.L. Fleeger (1995), 'Case studies for method and tool evaluation', *IEEE Software*, July, 52–62.

Leenders, M.R. and J.A. Erskine (1978), *Case Research and the Case Writing Process*, 2nd edition, London, Ontario: Research and Publications Division, School of Business Administration, The University of Western Ontario.

MacDonald, B. and R. Walker (1975), 'Case study and the social philosophy of educational research', *Cambridge Journal of Education*, **5**(1), 2–11.

McLeod, J. (1979), *Clinical Examination*, Edinburgh: Churchill Livingstone.

Patton, E. and S.H. Appelbaum (2003), 'The case for case studies in management research', *Management Research News*, **26**(5), 60–71.

Simons, H. (1996), 'The paradox of case study', *Cambridge Journal of Education*, **26**(2), 225–40.

Yin, R.K. (1984), *Case Study Research: Design and Methods*, 1st edition, Newbury Park, CA: Sage.

Yin, R.K. (1989), *Case Study Research: Design and Methods*, revised edition, Thousand Oaks, CA: Sage.

Yin, R.K. (1994), *Case Study Research, Design and Methods*, 2nd edition, Thousand Oaks, CA: Sage.

Yin, R.K. (2009), *Case Study Research: Design and Methods*, 4th edition, Thousand Oaks, CA: Sage.

 OTHER SUGGESTED READING

Adler, P.S., B. Goldaftas, and D.I. Levine (1999), 'Flexibility versus efficiency: A case study of model changeovers in the Toyota Production System', *Organization Science*, **10**(1), 46–68.

Franklin, R.D., D.B. Allison, and B.S. Gorman (eds) (1997), *Design and Analysis of Single-Case Designs*, Mahwah, NJ: Lawrence Erlbaum Associates.

George, A.L. and A. Bennett (2005), *Case Studies and Theory Development*, Cambridge, MA: MIT Press.

Gerring, J. (2007), *Case Study Research: Principles and Practices*, Cambridge, UK: Cambridge University Press.

Guercini, S. (2004), 'Developing the researcher–manager interface in the case analysis process', *Management Decision*, **42**(3/4), 464–72.

Hershen, M. and D.H. Barlow (1976), *Single Case Study Experimental Designs: Studies for Studying Behavioral Change*, Oxford: Pergamon Press.

Kazdin, A.E. (1982), *Single Case Research Designs*, Oxford: Oxford University Press.

Ragin, C.C. and H.S. Becker (eds) (1992), *What is a Case? Exploring the Foundations of Social Inquiry*, New York: Cambridge University Press.

2

Identifying motivation, objective, questions, and unit of analysis

> Answers are easy. It's the questions that are the challenge.
> (Paraphrase of Sherlock Holmes on a *Mystery Woman*, date unknown)

 LEARNING OBJECTIVES

In this chapter we focus on responding to the following four questions:

1 What is our motivation for undertaking the research?

2 What is the purpose of the research?

3 What is/are the research question/s?

4 What is the unit of analysis?

These four important questions begin our adventure, a journey into the complex, and often ambiguous, process of case study research.

2.1 What is our motivation for undertaking the research?

Why are you personally undertaking the research? Understanding ourselves is a very critical first step. Our personal motivation has a great deal to do with (1) the time, energy, effort, and creative powers we are willing to invest in the research project or program; (2) identification of biases in many aspects of the research process; and (3) our willingness to pursue lateral investigations that might help explain our phenomenon or lead to future research interests.

A research project is usually shorter term in nature – for example, a design involving one or more case studies aimed at publication of a report or an article. A research program, in contrast, is usually longer term in nature. A research program usually consists of multiple projects and could stretch to a decade or more, or even a career lifetime. A research program will probably result in multiple reports or articles and perhaps a book (or two or three!). The written output transmits the data accumulated and the learning acquired as the research progresses. In contrast, a project will take effort over a shorter period of time, perhaps a month or, in some instances, more sustained over multiple months.

The issue of personal motivation is seldom explicitly discussed. However, taking some time to reflect on our personal reasons for undertaking the research is a good investment, because personal motivation and circumstances can affect the selection of every facet of the research process.

Taking time to consider our personal interest and circumstances can help us be realistic about what we can undertake in the project, or whether we have a sustained interest that might lead to a longer-term program. Understanding your personal motivation will help you be realistic about the level of effort you are willing to put in. It will also help to understand the types of research foci and settings that you are willing to be involved in, or those that you definitely *do not* want to be involved with. *Understanding your personal reason for undertaking a project or a program of any research is important to understanding these issues.*

Individual motivations underlying research tend to fall into two categories: (1) initiation by an external person such as an instructor or a boss; and (2) personal interest. We explain each below.

External initiation

A class requirement is often a major external impetus for student research. We have supervised many such class projects. These include courses that have involved consulting projects, action research, problem-based learning, and service learning. Such courses often require an end-of-project report, which involves a process similar to the case study research that is the focus of this book. We are particularly interested in providing guidance for projects, theses or dissertation requirements that rely on case research methodology. But, the advice within these pages is equally valid for other kinds of educational programs or course requirements that require research involving a case study.

Case research associated with class requirements may take on aspects of action research that we cover in Chapter 4. Initiation of a research project may also come from the intrinsic nature of the individual's job. The US Government Accountability Office (GAO) has, for example, analysts who regularly design and carry out policy studies. The studies may be mandated by law such as an evaluation of the effect of a change in the law. In other instances US Congress committees that are considering the possibility of putting forward a bill or changes in existing laws may request a study.

GAO lead analyst Susan Iott [sic] explained various challenges she confronted in designing the study of federal land management agencies' use of ecosystem management. One challenge she found was that 'the underlying policy problem was unclear and thus difficult to operationalize in a study. The term ecosystem management was used broadly by federal agencies' (2010, p. 290). Ultimately Ms. Iott resolved that her job, that is, her motivation for taking on the challenge, required 'identifying the policy problem at hand and designing an approach to study it, informing the requesters about it, and providing a final report. . .that describes the problem and potential solution, as well as meeting the needs of the client' (2010, p. 291). We will return to this specific example later in this chapter to demonstrate how analyst Iott met the challenges of her assignment.

In other instances the individual may be a member of a firm that wants to demonstrate an achievement or successful completion of a project to its peer companies. The individual may be asked to write a case study of what the firm views as an exemplar to demonstrate the firm's capabilities to customers. We have not used these examples in this book because (1) the 'research' tends to be biased; and (2) the rigor of the research process is often lacking. The research is biased because too often the writer is expected to include data and information that puts the firm in a favorable light. In other instances the writer may be pressured to provide a more positive interpretation than the data warrants. Further, deadlines often place pressures on the author to short-change on the depth of research. In the field of journalism a somewhat different set of circumstances may occur. The reporter may be charged to find a story that will help to sell copies. Such stories often have a negative slant. These kinds of situations lead to the occasional criticism of case research: 'That's "just" journalism!' This book is devoted to avoiding that criticism. What you will learn in this book will help you evaluate reports and articles regarding their trustworthiness.

Personal interest, experiences, and circumstances

Throughout our careers, students have approached us with a request that starts with something like, 'Would you be willing to supervise a for-credit project for me? I'm interested in. . .'. Sometimes these requests are for a thesis or a dissertation. Sometimes the request is for an independent study. Requests for an independent study sometimes start with something like, 'I need one more hour of credit to graduate. I thought perhaps I could study. . .'. Another variation is 'I would like to start my own business within a couple of years of graduation and I'd like to. . .'. While these latter examples are not case study research per se, the process is similar. Often implied in these conversations is the expectation of a top grade. Frankly, we have often rejoined by pointing out that a well-done independent study often takes twice as much time and effort as a 'regular' class. After hearing our expectations, it is not unusual for a student to seek out another professor! But, in some instances, these investigations have led to the development of award-winning case studies.

Other instances are personal experiences. For example, author Taylor taught a course in organizational behavior while she was still a doctoral student. One module in the course focused on concepts relating to power and influence in organizations. The class materials included readings, a case, and experiential exercises. An undergraduate student who was employed in a local company stopped by after class to ask some questions about the course. As the conversation came to a conclusion, Taylor asked the student, 'Well, tell me, in your job how [given the class content] will you exercise power and influence?' The immediate reply was, 'Well, when I get a promotion, I'll have power and then I can exercise influence'.

Taylor was surprised and disappointed – the student had completely missed major points in the material, which included insights about how people without formal power could acquire and exercise influence. The incident initiated her intense study of the power and influence sub-field and gave initial impetus for her doctoral dissertation research. The dissertation utilized case study research methodology and focused on individuals whose positions were not endowed with significant direct power. The question that guided the research was how such individuals influenced whole system change.

Researchers may provide insights into what motivated their interest in a research issue in a book foreword. However, researchers seldom indicate their personal motivation in journal articles.

A very pragmatic reason for using a case study approach to research may be the orientation of the educational institution where a student is enrolled. Some schools have long-term orientations toward qualitative research such as a case study process. Other schools emphasize quantitative approaches to research methodology. Some encourage a blend or accept either as equally valid methodological approaches.

One excellent description of personal motivation comes from University of Twente researcher Petra de Weerd-Nederhof (2001) who wrote intimately about her graduate thesis design and process. Among other issues she pointed out her school's orientation toward qualitative studies, her own lack of skills with quantitative techniques, and her lack of business experience. All of these dimensions of her background contributed to her choice of qualitative design that took her inside the organizations she studied. Weerd-Nederhof studied new product development processes. The experience of observing the processes first-hand gave her opportunity to develop an experience background that would not have been so readily possible if she had used a more arm's-length approach such as a survey or meta-analysis of others' articles.

In short, understanding our personal motivations and reasons for undertaking our methodological approach can be a wise investment of time and effort. As noted in the above examples, personal experiences and interests, the orientation of the institution you are associated with, and your own personal skills may contribute to the choice of methodology.

2.2   What is the purpose of the research?

Establishing the objective of the study can be an exciting phase. This phase is the dreaming stage, unlike some of the other stages or phases that are more mechanical. It consists of expressing the underlying purpose of the study explicitly. This phase answers questions such as: What is the *purpose* of our research? What are we *really* interested in understanding? Table 2.1 provides four examples of research purpose statements, one each from the fields of strategic management, corporate social responsibility (CSR), health care administration, and quality management.

All of the examples in Table 2.1 are explicit regarding the purpose of the study. In other instances the purpose may be explicit, but it may be scattered in the article. In the following example, we pulled from two different points in the article to provide a purpose statement:

> Career Management/Psychology: [Our study focuses on. . .] mechanisms related to career progression. . . [In particular]. . .situations in which traumatic life events necessitate a discontinuous career transition are becoming increasingly prevalent . . . [The study focuses on]. . .career constraints and on how individuals adapt to new careers (Haynie and Shepherd, 2011, p. 501).

Table 2.1 Examples of research objective or purpose statements

Field	Stated objective or purpose
Strategic management	The objective of this paper is to contribute to a better understanding of the sources of the competitiveness of firms in the fashion and luxury goods industry (Donzé, 2012, p. 115)
Corporate social responsibility (CSR)	The purpose of this study is to improve our understanding of corporate social responsiveness by examining the relationship between corporate responsiveness strategy and stakeholders (Lee, 2007, p. 219)
Health care administration	This article aims to examine the implementation process of diagnosis-related groups (DRGs) in the clinical departments of a German hospital group and to explain why some gain competitive advantage while others do not (Ridder, Doege, and Martini, 2007, p. 2120)
Quality management	This paper aims to explore the implementation of the 5Ss[a] in multinational organizations in Mexico empirically, in order to analyze and compare them against the respective theoretical frameworks (Suárez-Barraza and Ramis-Pujol, 2012, p. 77)

Note: a. 5S is the name of a workplace organization method that uses a list of five Japanese words: *seiri* (sort), *seiton* (set in order), *seiso* (shine), *seiketsu* (standardize), and *shitsuke* (sustain).

As we noted earlier, US GAO policy analyst Susan Iott struggled with aspects of her assignment. After resolving the purpose or objective, she sought to define the basic problem or the overarching purpose of the study and, as we will track in Chapter 3, the design of the study. To understand the committee's purpose in requesting the study, she explained that she needed 'some further context'. As part of developing the context she considered a number of aspects of the situation including (1) multiple goals, (2) trends, and (3) mitigating factors. Ultimately she identified a 'problem statement'. The problem or question was to develop an understanding of how various land management programs resolved 'conflict among multiple landowners with different land management goals [thus]. . . Our study needed to focus on a successful way to define the common interest in the face of conflicting interests and multiple, fragmented land ownerships' (lott, 2010, p. 295).

Why are some researchers so very specific about the purpose of their studies while others, as in Iott's example above, are more oblique? Part of the answer comes from the requirements of the journal in which the article is published. If the journal requires an explicit statement, the researcher will produce one. In the example above the journal did not.

A thesis or dissertation is very likely to include a research purpose or objective since the faculty supervisor generally asks something like, 'What is it you want to study?' or 'Why don't we take a look at. . .?' Either question is a step in the journey that involves establishing the purpose, deriving the research questions, and identifying of the unit of analysis.

Another example is Coates (2004). At the time, her graduate school, Rensselaer Polytechnic Institute (RPI) in Troy, New York, had a major grant to study the process by which new technologies were generated within companies. The interests of her RPI faculty were focused on understanding processes. In addition, Coates had been part-owner in a small, but avant-garde, software company. She had worked with the software designers to get them to adapt the company's software packages to the needs of her customers. Coates chose RPI deliberately because of her interests in technologies and the processes of bringing them to market. No wonder that she explained that her research 'explores the innovation process of new-to-the-world technologies by examining the activities undertaken at the project level. Grounded in the resource based view of the firm, this study examines the process of emerging technological innovation' (Coates, 2004, Abstract, n.p.).

The purposes of most of the case research examples above are primarily descriptive or exploratory in nature. Exploratory research is generally intended to generate propositions or hypotheses for further study. There are, however, instances in which case research is used for other purposes. As Box 2.1 depicts, research purposes can be descriptive, exploratory, and confirmatory[1] in nature. These purposes form a continuum that is associated with the possibilities of testing propositions or preliminary hypotheses.

Bonoma (1985) provides a somewhat different continuum of research purposes. Bonoma's five-phase scheme includes: (1) description, (2) classification, (3) measurement/estimation, (4) establishing of association, and (5) determining cause and effect (Bonoma, 1985, p. 201). The categories are essentially the same as those we depicted in Box 2.1. The important issue is that the continuum moves from (1) description to (5) determining cause and effect (or from descriptive to testing of propositions/preliminary hypotheses). These and the interim phases are rough steps in an entire process of moving from description of a phenomenon to determining the causal paths among the various variables that have been discovered in the process of the investigation. The early part of the process is generally inductive in nature. Thus, we can say a phenomenon has to be described. Its components require classification before they can be measured or estimated. The data may or may not suggest associations among the various components of the situation. If associations are identified, which precedes the other is important to ascertain. A second set of issues relates to whether

THE CONTINUUM OF CASE RESEARCH PURPOSES

Descriptive	Generation of theory	Affirmatory	Test propositions/ preliminary hypotheses
The comparative study of two British football teams gave the researchers the opportunity to explore and describe the knowledge management processes within each team (Doloriert and Whitworth, 2011).	This grounded theory study of three open source projects was focused on generating theory about the organizational outcomes emanating from adoption of open sourcing (Allen and Geller, 2012).	The extent of theory development in the field of entrepreneurship and human resources permits an affirmatory oriented analysis for this case study. The analysis is iterative –that is, the authors move between the case study itself and the extant theories (Ki-Hoon, 2007).	This seven-case study design focused on identifying the factors that affect the viability of electronic marketplaces. Three of the cases were descriptive while four were used for theory building (Iacona et al., 2011).[a]

Note: a. This article is more about an audit trail of the research than it is about the research itself.

Table 2.2 Classification of case studies

Role of researcher	Type of case study				
	A-theoretical case study	Hypotheses-generating case study	Interpreting case study	Theory-testing case study	Deviating case study
Relates to known deviation from theory or to critical case				No	Yes
Critical or testing of theory			No	Yes	
Relates to known theory about the field of the social problem	No	No	Yes		
As point of departure seeks to identify the social problem through transformation to case terminology	No	Yes			

Source: Pedersen (1977, p. 251) (table originally in Danish, translated and reversed).

the precedent event is necessary for the subsequent to occur. If so there is indication of a causal link.

The choice that the researcher makes with respect to the relationship between theory and case material is another defining dimension of the type of case study. Case and theory are linked concepts. According to Pedersen, 'a case is always a case of something'. What Pedersen means is that the term 'case' cannot be used without assuming the existence or the possibility of some kind of theory (1977, p. 243). Pedersen (1977, p. 244) points at five different ways of categorizing case studies. These five classifications are listed in Table 2.2, which also indicates the role of the researcher in defining the relationship between the purpose of the case study and the type of the case study.

First, a-theoretical case studies contain unique phenomena that are not related to any existing social theory. The term is often considered a contradiction to Pedersen's earlier comment above (Pedersen, 1977, p. 244). Second, interpretative case studies attempt to understand a unique phenomenon by using an existing valid theory. The case serves as an illustration of the theory. Third, a theory-testing case study tends to test, refine or modify or falsify known theoretical propositions the validity of which is not taken for granted. Fourth, deviating or critical case studies serve to test, refine or modify an existing theory. Further this type of case study is used when the researcher seeks to examine special critical situations that the theory has to be able to explain in order to maintain its validity. Fifth, in the case study that aims at generating theory or hypotheses a unique phenomenon will be studied 'clinically'. The search is to identify empirical relations that will provide the basis for generalizations that expand the validity of the theory – moving beyond what was previously included in the theory.

2.3   What is/are the research question/s?

From the purpose statement one can see a natural progression to the research questions (Table 2.3). However, the close match between purpose on one hand and questions on the other belies the interactive effort that led to the synchronization of the two.

In some instances the research purpose and the research question appear to be identical, one rendered as a statement and the other in question form. In other instances, the purpose is expressed as a desire to develop deeper understanding of a broader phenomenon or set of phenomena. The research questions focus more sharply on what might be possible to investigate within the limitations of time and resources.

One contrasting example, of course, is Iott. Using the process above, Iott identified the research question as how successful programs found ways to 'define the common interest in the face of conflicting interests and multiple, fragmented land ownerships' (2010, p. 295). Iott's next challenge was to identify the unit of analysis, an issue that is the focus of the next section.

As will be noted from Table 2.3 'why' and 'how' questions tend to dominate in case research. Most case researchers concur that these are the appropriate kinds of questions to guide such investigations (Kitchenham, Pitchard, and Fleeger, 1995, p. 52).

2.4   What is the unit of analysis?

The unit of analysis refers to the subject that is the focus of the study. The author of one well-known book refers to the unit of analysis as the 'study object' (Stake, 1995, p. 3). The choice of unit of analysis or study object follows from the motivation, purpose, and questions. A major issue is identifying the boundary between the unit of analysis and its context. Is the researcher focusing on a single cell or its components, an individual person, a small group, an organization, a city, a region, a country, or a solar system? (See the Appendix to this chapter for examples of case studies at various levels.) A related issue is whether the research is focused on the unit itself or on a process within a unit. By definition a process usually involves study over time, either by observations taken at different points in time or through historical accounts gathered verbally or through documentation.

If the focus is on the unit, then the historical information may provide context to help the researcher and the audience for the manuscript to understand the unit at the point in time at which it is studied. If the focus is on a process, then the unit (an individual or organization, for example) and perhaps its history provide the context.

Ambiguity is an issue that challenges all case research. Reducing the ambiguity is important. Clarifying the definition of the unit of analysis under investigation makes a significant contribution toward reducing the inherent ambiguity and improving the generalizability claims of the study. Multiple authors argue that the unit of analysis and the case itself are synonymous (e.g., Miles and Huberman, 1994, p. 25; Patton and Appelbaum, 2003; Grünbaum, 2007). We note that they are indeed very similar. The difference is that the case is a description of the unit of analysis *and* its context.

Not everyone fully agrees. On one hand, Yin makes clear the importance of identifying the unit of analysis under study when he says: 'A major step in designing and conducting a single case is defining the unit of analysis (or the case itself)' (2004, p. 44). But, Grünbaum takes a different view. Grünbaum, in essence, tends to concur with Yin's acceptance of the case and unit of analysis as synonymous, but points out that Yin begins to waiver when more than one case make up the study design. Thus, Grünbaum argues that only under certain circumstances are the case and the unit of analysis clearly separated. His arguments help us understand that if one does not have the first unit of analysis clearly identified, identifying a priori subsequent theoretically comparable units will be clearly inefficient and probably ineffective as

Table 2.3 Research purpose and associated research questions

Research purpose	Associated research question(s)
Abstract: This study *explores*[a] the process of global sourcing through a case of the Swedish furnishing retailer IKEA from an interaction perspective The *purpose* of this paper is to *contribute to the understanding* of the global sourcing process by applying the interaction approach as a theoretical lens (Hultman et al., 2012, p. 9)	Abstract: With a point of departure in the streams of existing research on global sourcing and the internationalization process of firms through networks, a *research question* is proposed concerning supply network interactions as an influence in the global sourcing process. . .[Hence this] gives rise to the following research question: How do supply network interactions influence the global sourcing process? (Hultman et al., 2012, p. 10)
Abstract*: Purpose*. . .this paper aims to *explore* the implementation of the 5Ss[b] in multinational organizations in Mexico empirically, in order to analyze and compare them against the respective theoretical frameworks For this reason, the *main purpose* of this study is to empirically explore 5S implementation in multinational organizations in Mexico with the aim of analyzing and comparing it with theoretical frameworks on the subject (Suárez-Barraza and Ramis-Pujol, 2012, p. 79)	Abstract: The *research question* that governs the study is: 'How are the 5Ss implemented in an organizational context such as that of a multinational company in Mexico?' More specifically, we seek to answer the main research question of the study, namely: How does 5S implementation take place in an organizational context such as a multinational corporation in Mexico? This is achieved through three specific sub-questions: RQ1.1: Why do multinational organizations in Mexico need to implement 5S? In other words, what are its main drivers? RQ1.2: What sort of inhibitors can arise in 5S implementation in multinational organizations in Mexico? RQ1.3: Is there any relationship between the 5S implementation effort and the general Lean thinking and *Kaizen* programs and/or projects of each multinational organization? (Suárez-Barraza and Ramis-Pujol, 2012, p. 79)
Thus, in our study, we investigate the implementation process of diagnosis-related groups (DRGs) in a German hospital group. Our *aim* is to present findings on how clinical departments implement DRGs and why some gain competitive advantage while others do not (Ridder et al., 2007, p. 2122)	Our *research questions* can be described as follows: (1) Change resources: How do hospitals accumulate and develop change resources in order to implement DRGs? (2) Path: How does the existing path of a hospital influence the implementation of DRGs?

Table 2.3 (continued)

Research purpose	Associated research question(s)
[Note: This purpose statement suggests beginning hypotheses that differentiate between successful and unsuccessful implementation processes.]	(3) Processes: How do hospitals develop new routines through processes of coordination, learning, and reconfiguration in order to implement DRGs? (4) Implementation outcomes leading to competitive advantage: How do clinical departments develop competencies in DRG coding, patient treatment processes, and specialization? Overall, we expect that idiosyncratic patterns among clinical departments exist in each category, which will lead to specific implementation processes (Eisenhardt and Martin, 2000; Ridder et al., 2007, pp. 2124–5) [Note: Original is flowing text.]
This dissertation *explores* connections between the evolution of the research mission at Wayne State and Cleveland State Universities and forces in their external environment, especially competitors, accrediting agencies, and state and federal governments, in the context of the post-World War II era (Kidder, 2007, p. 157)	The primary *research question* is: what factors influenced the emergence of two urban state universities and the evolution of their missions in the post-World War II era? The study contributes a historical perspective on 'academic drift': here, the development of a research mission at these institutions, members of a significantly under-researched sector of American higher education (Kidder, 2007, p. 158)

Notes:
a. Italics added in all instances.
b. 5S is the name of a workplace organization method that uses a list of five Japanese words: *seiri* (sort), *seiton* (set in order), *seiso* (shine), *seiketsu* (standardize), and *shitsuke* (sustain).

well. Grünbaum (2007) asks whether it is possible: 'to transfer results from just one case to other contexts? Additionally, it is now crystallized what it is the researcher wants to transfer because the case and the unit of analysis are clearly detached' (2007, p. 87).

Notwithstanding the controversies, the issue is an important one. Is the case the unit of analysis? We argue 'No' given the definition of a case as a description of the relevant factors related to the unit of analysis *and* its context. That said, we reiterate that one of the key issues with case research is where the boundary between the unit of analysis and its context truly lies.[2]

Figure 2.1 The rational approach to research preliminaries: sequential relationship

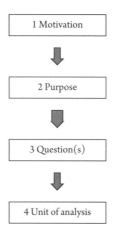

However, 'spinning our wheels' or spending excess time on the issue of where the boundary lies early in a case study project is probably not a good use of our time. Gerring, who articulated the purpose of case studies for the field of political science, noted that although the temporal boundaries of a unit are not always explicit, authors make them implicit (2004, p. 342). At the same time, improving the definition of what we are studying – the unit of analysis – is important and must not be neglected. After all, if we don't clearly understand what we have studied, how can we claim that the situation is like or unlike others not yet studied?

But, what is a 'unit of analysis'? As we suggested, the unit of analysis can vary widely from single cell to the solar system. Generally, in the field of management, the unit of analysis is something 'in between'. For example, Christensen and Carlile point out that:

> [t]he unit of analysis of a case may be a national economy, an industry, a period of trading on a stock exchange, a population of patients, a single patient, a company, a set of projects, the career experiences of a population of people, or a single experience of an individual. All are cases and all examine data that are subjective abstractions or manifestations of much more complex underlying reality (Christensen and Carlile, 2009, p. 243).

Gerring put it well when he said: 'A unit connotes a spatially bounded phenomenon, e.g., a nation-state, revolution, political party, election, or person – observed at a single point in time or over some delimited period of time' (2004, p. 342). We note, however, that within the social sciences, of which business studies is a part, the focus is on people and the organizational systems that they construct and inhabit. What we are discussing here, then, is how we go about defining and establishing that unit of analysis.

Caveats regarding the unit of analysis

We argue that the definition of the unit of analysis must be carefully defined before beginning the study. At the same time, we recognize two difficulties. First, as we pointed out earlier, the boundary between the unit of analysis and its context may be murky. Second, the boundaries of the research may shift during the course of the research.

An investigation usually begins with the expectation that the phenomenon may be reasonably understood within the boundaries established. However, in case study research we are studying that phenomenon in situ or within its situation or context. The next level in the system is often observed to have sufficient impact that it must be included in the study so that the researcher can assert that the case description and subsequent explanations are trustworthy.

This observation helps us to understand that case study methodology recognizes the system nature of any unit of analysis. Where to draw the boundaries of the system under study is often a matter of practicality, including limits on time and resources. We also note that such 'systems think' can too easily lead to 'scope creep'. Certainly the negative implications of scope creep constitute one reason why more than one graduate student has avoided faculty who advocate case study methodology. As one of our graduate students approaching dissertation stage put it, 'I don't want to do a case-based research dissertation. I want to get finished!' However, faculty members do recognize this issue, as an article by Perry (1998) indicates. Perry tracked eight students who used a case study approach. Three were Master's-level students and five were PhD students. Perry was careful to note that 'all completed their thesis within normal time' (np) with no or few committee-required changes. Further there were publication streams accruing from the research work.

However, case study research does pose issues in terms of timely completion. Indeed, it is the underlying reason why one of our dissertation committee members, whom we will call 'Professor Smith', declined to chair the committee. Professor Smith had been the first one on the faculty to urge the study of the phenomenon, but he declined to chair the investigation. He explained that in the past his personal curiosity had led to continuing expansion of the boundaries of the research. Professor Smith stated: 'I caused my last doctoral student to almost not graduate. I don't want to do that to you!' Professor Smith was what we might deem as curious, always wanting to explore beyond the boundaries of the information already known! We can criticize, but good scholars are personally curious. Thus, as they accumulate information about the phenomenon, they see additional questions, issues and nuances that would be fruitful for study – or at least 'just' intrinsically interesting. Resisting the urge of the resulting 'scope creep' takes discipline and it is like dieting – not easy!

There are often good reasons for our interest in broadening what is included in a case. We might want to study a case simply because the case is interesting. The classic case study author Stake (1995) referred to such cases as 'intrinsic', meaning they are of interest in and of themselves and the investigator has no interest in generalizing beyond the situation. A second reason is to understand the phenomenon and its context before proceeding with the study of a broader sample. This reason often underlies a graduate student's interest in a case study.

2.5   A final word

But, which really comes first – the personal motivation, establishment of the objective of the study, derivation of the research questions, or the identification of the unit of analysis? From a strictly rational, logical point of view the motivation comes first, establishing the purpose next, the research question follows, and finally the unit of analysis. Indeed, our discussion in this chapter implies that there is a sequential relationship among these four as suggested in Figure 2.1. In reality, the relationship is as depicted in Figure 2.2. The truth of the matter is that the four are inextricably linked. You can start with any of the four. A rational approach suggests Figure 2.1. Reality acknowledges Figure 2.2. These four, along with other aspects of the research that we discuss in Chapters 3 and 4, are integrative, synergistic, and mutually

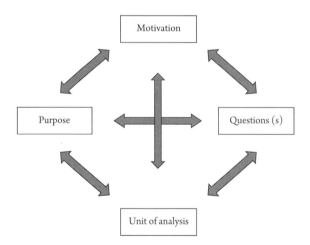

Figure 2.2 The reality of the relationships

influential. You might start a conversation with an advisor that opens with something like 'I'm really interested in. . .' or 'I'd really like to study. . .' – that is, a discussion of the purpose. On the other hand, a research project might start with a remark such as 'That's a really interesting situation!' or 'The CEO of Angles, Inc. indicated she is open to research involving her company'. Regardless of where you might start in the process, it is highly likely that as you move forward you will find that other aspects of the study are fluid and subject to change.

 END OF CHAPTER QUESTIONS AND ANSWERS

You may start with any of the four questions. The questions were asked and answered in the following order in Chapter 2:

1 **What is our motivation for undertaking the research?** Both external and personally derived motivation relate to some of the mysteries of undertaking case study research. Such motivations influence parts of the case research in many ways. It is thus wise to spend some time clarifying your motivations for doing the case research. Among the reasons that we have encountered that have influenced individuals to undertake specific research were a personal experience or interest, an individual's own personal skills contributing to the choice of methodology and/or the orientation of the institution with which the person was associated.

2 **What is the research objective?** The purpose of a case research study is developing an understanding of a phenomenon and its context. Formulating explicitly what you really are interested in understanding is part of the process that leads to the development of the research question/s.

3 **What is/are the research question/s?** Research objectives can usually be formulated as a statement. However, the research question should be rendered in question format. Research questions are questions that focus on what might be possible to investigate within given limits of time and other resources.

4 **What is the unit of analysis?** It is what is interesting. It is the subject and focus of the study. It is what you what to understand. The unit of analysis is not the case. A case is the unit of analysis in its context. The choice of unit of analysis or study object follows from the motivation, purpose, and questions. It is the object of your study. It can be a single cell, or a system. Is what is interesting the unit or the process?

NOTES

1 Confirmatory research reviews prior research that has demonstrated some aspect of the phenomenon. The researcher uses the current effort to reaffirm, or question, prior findings. See, for example, Marodin and Saurin (2015) and Faes and Matthyssens (2009). Generally, an output from a qualitative case study is followed by confirmatory research of a different nature, such as a survey. See, for example, Rudolph and Emrich (2009).

2 For example, cases involving interconnecting systems may pose the most difficulty in defining the unit of analysis. See the following articles: (1) Hinkka, Främling, and Tätilä (2013): In this instance the unit of analysis was 'network of supplier and wholesaler (buyer) companies acting in the Finnish technical trade industry, which are implementing inter-organizational tracking' (p. 1133). (2) Velden and Lagoze (2013): The unit of analysis that Velden and Lagoze chose was even more complicated as the unit of analysis was scientific communities or networks of scientists and sub-communities. These authors pointed out that it

was 'a challenging unit of analysis to capture and compare because they overlap, have fuzzy boundaries, and evolve over time. We describe a network analytic approach that reveals the complexities of these communities through the examination of their publication networks in combination with insights from ethnographic field studies. We suggest that the structures revealed indicate overlapping sub-communities within a research specialty, and we provide evidence that they differ in disciplinary orientation and research practices' (Velden and Lagoze, 2013, Abstract).

REFERENCES

Allen, J.P. and D. Geller (2012), 'Open source deployment in local government: Rapid innovation as an occasion for revitalizing organizational IT', *Information Technology & People*, **25**(2), 136–55.

Anyansi-Archibong, C. (2010), 'Entrepreneurship as a critical and missing factor in economic development of poor nations: A systematic analysis of factors of production', *IUP Journal of Business Strategy*, **7**(1), 7–20.

Atsu, M.Y., F. Andoh-Baidoo, B. Osatuyi, and K. Amoako-Gyampah (2010), 'An exploratory study of the contextual factors that influence success of ICT projects in developing nations: A case study of a telecommunications company in Ghana', *Journal of Information Technology Case and Application Research*, **12**(3), 56–81.

Bonoma, T.V. (1985), 'Case research in marketing: Opportunities, problems, and a process', *Journal of Marketing Research*, **22**(2), 199–208.

Christensen, C.L. and P.R. Carlile (2009), 'Course research: Using case method to build and teach management theory', *Academy of Management Learning & Education*, **8**(2), 240–51.

Coates, T.L. (2004), 'The development of core competence through emerging technology innovation: An empirical investigation', doctoral dissertation, Rensselaer Polytechnic Institute (private transmission).

De Weerd-Nederhof, P.C. (2001), 'Qualitative case study research. The case of a PhD research project on organising and managing new product development systems', *Management Decision*, **39**(7), 513–38.

Doloriert, C. and K. Whitworth (2011), 'A case study of knowledge management in the "back office" of two English football clubs', *The Learning Organization*, **18**(6), 422–37.

Donzé, P.-Y. (2012), 'The comeback of the Swiss watch industry on the world market: A business history of the Swatch Group (1983–2010)', *Journal of Strategic Management Education*, **8**(2), 115–46.

Eisenhardt, K.M. and J.A. Martin (2000), 'Dynamic capabilities: What are they?' *Strategic Management Journal*, **21**(10/11), 1105–21.

Faes, W. and P. Matthyssens (2009), 'Insights into the process of changing sourcing strategies', *The Journal of Business & Industrial Marketing*, **24**(3/4), 245–55.

Ferriani, S., E. Garnsey, and G. Lorenzoni (2012), 'Continuity and change in a spin-off venture: The process of reimprinting', *Industrial and Corporate Change*, **21**(4), 1011–48.

Gerring, J. (2004), 'What is a case study and what is it good for?' *The American Political Science Review*, **98**(2), 341–54.

Grünbaum, N.N. (2007), 'Identification of ambiguity in the case study research typology: So what is a unit of analysis?' *Qualitative Market Research*, **10**(1), 78–97.

Haynie, J.M. and D. Shepherd (2011), 'Toward a theory of discontinuous career transition: Investigating career transitions necessitated by traumatic life events', *Journal of Applied Psychology*, **96**(3), 501–24.

Hinkka, V., K. Främling, and J. Tätilä (2013), 'Supply chain tracking: Aligning buyer and supplier incentives', *Industrial Management + Data Systems*, **113**(8), 1133–48.

Hultman, J., R. Johnsen, T. Johnsen, and S. Hertz (2012), 'An interaction approach to global sourcing: A case study of IKEA', *Journal of Purchasing & Supply Management*, **18**(1), 9–21.

Iacona, A., M.G. Raso, R.B. Canani, A. Calignano, and R. Meli (2011), 'Probiotics as an emerging therapeutic strategy to treat NAFLD: Focus on molecular and biochemical mechanisms', *Journal of Nutritional Biochemistry*, **22**(8), 699–711.

Iott, S. (2010), 'Practitioner insights: Policy sciences and congressional research: Making sense of the research question', *Policy Sciences*, **43**(3), 289–300.

Kidder, R.D. (2007), 'The evolution of research mission in urban state universities in post-World War II America: A comparative case study (Michigan, Ohio)', in R. Geiger (ed.), *Perspectives on the History of Higher Education, Vol. 26*, New Brunswick, NJ: Transaction Publishers.

Ki-Hoon, L. (2007), 'Corporate social responsiveness in the Korean electronics industry', *Corporate Social Responsibility and Environmental Management*, **14**(4), 219–30.

Kitchenham, B., L. Pitchard, and S.L. Fleeger (1995), 'Case studies for method and tool evaluation', *IEEE Software*, July, 52–62.

Kurnia, S. and R.B. Johnston (2006), 'A dynamic international model of inter-organization system adoption: The case of category management adoption in Australia', *Asia Pacific Management Review*, 11(1), accessed 15 March 2017 at http://apmr.management.ncku.edu.tw/abstract.asp?id=131.

Lee, K.-H. (2007), 'Corporate social responsiveness in the Korean electronics industry', *Corporate Social Responsibility and Environmental Management*, **14**(4), 219–30.

Marodin, G.A. and T.A. Saurin (2015), 'Classification and relationships between risks that affect lean production implementation: A study in southern Brazil', *Journal of Manufacturing Technology Management*, **26**(1), 79–59.

Miles, M.B. and A.M. Huberman (1994), *Qualitative Data Analysis: An Expanded Sourcebook*, 2nd edition, Thousand Oaks, CA: Sage.

Muralidhar, K. (2010), 'Enterprise risk management in the Middle East oil industry', *International Journal of Energy Sector Management*, **4**(1), 59–86.

Patton, E. and S.H. Appelbaum (2003), 'The case for case studies in management research', *Management Research News*, **26**(5), 60–71.

Pedersen, M.N. (1977), 'Om den rette brug af historiske materialer i statskundskaben' [On the appropriate use of historical materials in the field of political science], in E. Damgaard (ed.), *Festskrift til professor, Dr. Phil. Erik Rasmussen, 20. April 1977*, Aarhus: Politica.

Perry, C. (1998), 'Process of a case study methodology for postgraduate research in marketing', *European Journal of Marketing*, **32**(9/10), 785–802 (Source: http://search.proquest.com.proxy.library.umkc.edu/abicomplete/docview/237022454/fulltext/B261F229CD9E4C07PQ/1?accountid=14589; accessed March 31, 2017).

Ridder, H.G., V. Doege, and S. Martini (2007), 'Differences in the implementation of diagnosis-related groups across clinical departments: A German hospital case study', *Health Services Research*, **42**(6 Pt 1), 2120–39.

Rudolph, T. and O. Emrich (2009), 'Situation-related tasks for mobile services in retailing', *The International Review of Retail, Distribution and Consumer Research*, **19**(5), 483–503.

Stake, R. (1995), *The Art of Case Research*, Thousand Oaks, CA: Sage.

Suárez-Barraza, M.F. and J. Ramis-Pujol (2012), 'An exploratory study of 5S: A multiple case study of multinational organizations in Mexico', *Asian Journal on Quality*, **13**(1), 77–99.

Velden, T. and C. Lagoze (2013), 'The extraction of community structures from publication networks to support ethnographic observations of field differences in scientific communication', *Journal of the American Society for Information Science and Technology*, **64**(12), 2452–67.

Venugopal, C. and K.S. Rao (2011), 'Learning from a failed ERP implementation: A case study research', *International Journal of Managing Projects in Business*, **4**(4), 596–615.

Yin, R.K. (1994), *Case Study Research – Design and Method*, 2nd ed., Newbury Park, CA: Sage.

Appendix

Table 2A.1 Examples of and comments on various levels of units of analysis

Unit of analysis	Example
Nation	Most studies that consider a country look at a specific aspect of the country, such as implementation of ICT in the developing nation of Ghana. However, as with this study, while the purpose of the study may be to understand the issue within the country, the actual focus of the research is on one company (Atsu et al., 2010)
	In contrast, Anyansi-Archibong (2010) compared China and Nigeria. She used China's 7th National Development Plan and Nigeria's 5th National Development Plan as well as selected economic indicators as the data for the two case studies. She concluded that the Chinese emphasis on creating infrastructure promoted entrepreneurship and innovation activities within the country that had led to China 'far surpassing' Nigeria as a result of the former's country's entrepreneurial emphasis
Industry	Most are studies of companies within an industry – that is, designs involving small or large samples. One can find many histories of industries, but they are usually books or dissertations. An unusual study looks at the use of enterprise risk management (ERM) within the Middle East oil industry. The study includes six case studies from the oil industry in the six Gulf Cooperation Council (GCC) nations. The six nations are Bahrain, Kuwait, Oman, Qatar, Saudi Arabia, and United Arab Emirates. The purpose was to develop a plan for GCC oil and gas industry to fully develop ERM (Muralidhar, 2010)
Interorganizational relationships	This well-designed study of relationships considered the adoption of inter-organizational systems (IOS). The purpose was to improve supply chain efficiency, an issue that has proven to be difficult because it involves spanning organizational boundaries. The study utilized an interactional model to capture the reciprocal interactions between the firms that adopted IOS (Kurnia and Johnston, 2006)
Organization	The purpose of this study was an attempt to understand intergenerational learning and spin-off performance: the case study focused on Acorn computers and ARM semi-conductors. These two organizations formed the parent–progeny dyad that was the unit of analysis. The authors studied the micro-processes that led to the spin-off venture and the progeny's ability to continue useful practices from original parent and yet move forward to innovate (Ferriani et al., 2012)

Group	The purpose of this study was to discover how clinical departments in a hospital implemented the diagnosis-related groups (DRGs)[a] and, in doing so, why some gained competitive advantage while others did not (Ridder et al., 2007, p. 2122). The authors designed the study by choosing three successful departments and three unsuccessful departments. The primary source of data was interviews with participants internal to the hospital, but the researchers also used direct observation of monthly meetings and selected written documentation (Ridder et al., 2007, pp. 2120, 2127–8)
Individual	Some journals such as the *Journal of Applied Psychology* rarely publish case studies. However, this particular study was an exception in the history of this nearly 100-year-old journal. The two researchers focused on ten cases of individuals. Each case involved a member of the US military member who experienced combat trauma. The individuals who were the focus were discharged from military service because their injuries prevented the individuals from carrying out their military duties. In each instance, the individual participated in a retraining program that focused on entrepreneurship. The researchers investigated the individual's career previous to the injury, the events leading to the transition and its career and psychological implications, as well as the dynamics of the transition into the new career path (Haynie and Shepherd, 2011)
Process	This study focused on IKEA, a major Swedish furniture retailer and the supply network it developed with PAX wardrobe of China. The study focused on the process of developing IKEA's global sourcing process during the six-year period 2003–06 (Hultman et al., 2012)
Project	The purpose of the study was to understand how and why enterprise resource planning (ERP) projects failed to meet the expectations of the users. The unit of analysis was at the project level. The authors studied one successful and one failed project within the same organization. Their results suggested critical factors for success that could lead to successful implementation of such projects (Venugopal and Rao, 2011)

Note: a.   DRGs are a patient classification system that determined the level of reimbursement for hospital treatments of patients. DRGs were first initiated in the state of New Jersey, USA in 1980 and the usage spread to other states. A similar system was mandated beginning 2000 in Germany with the passage of the National Health Care Reform.

3

Choosing among case research designs

Since Hippocrates first presented 14 classic case studies of disease some 2300 years ago, science has proceeded along two divergent knowledge paths. One involves formulating a tentative theory of a phenomenon 'writ large,' deducing implied empirical consequences and controlling situational events in order to observe the validity of empirical deductions. The second path, less frequently used but equally valid, is to reason from individual and naturally occurring but largely uncontrollable observations toward generalizable inductive principles.

(Bonoma, 1985, p. 199)

LEARNING OBJECTIVES

In this chapter we explore the following six questions:

1 What are the stages in the research design process?

2 What options for research design are available for case study methodology?

3 How does the state of the literature impact on our choice?

4 When is case research *not* case research?

5 Which is better – qualitative data or quantitative data?

6 What is the 'right' research design?

3.1 What are the stages in the research design process?

The design of the study becomes the most important issue once we have identified the phenomenon that we want to study and the associated unit of

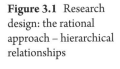

Figure 3.1 Research design: the rational approach – hierarchical relationships

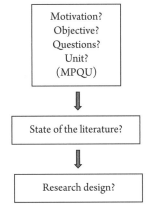

Figure 3.2 Research design: the reality of the relationships

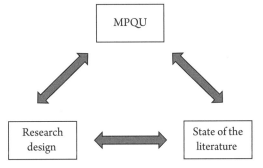

analysis. The study design or research methodology is not an isolated challenge. Rather, the choice of research methodology is integrally related to other issues in the overall research process.

The research design process does proceed through predictable stages, as Figure 3.1 suggests. However, the choice of research methodology is interactive with other issues, as Figure 3.2 demonstrates.

3.2 What options for research design are available for case study methodology?

There are many research designs available to investigate a phenomenon. As researchers we must make tradeoffs in selecting any particular research design. However, you should note that we might make a particular choice at one point in time during the process of the research and then find ourselves having to change that choice at a later point. Furthermore, expanding our knowledge about a phenomenon can involve using a variety of research approaches, either sequentially or even simultaneously.

The approaches to studying a phenomenon can be viewed as a continuum. At one end of the continuum are qualitative approaches such as case study methodology. These approaches generally use inductive or abductive reasoning approaches in comparison to the deductive reasoning that is generally used with more quantitative research. Christensen and Carlile (2009) articulate this issue well when they consider the links between case research methodology and approaches to teaching. The authors recount classroom experiences of teaching courses where the body of research and theoretical development is well developed and where it is not. They describe, for example, inductive and deductive approaches to course design and the classroom process where the group consisting of students and professor form, in essence, a research team.

Inductive

A course design that uses an inductive approach is more appropriate, Christensen and Carlile (2009) argue, where the theoretical development of the knowledge base underlying the course material is underdeveloped. In these instances the two authors suggest assigning a set of cases regarding the phenomenon. After several classes, the course pauses in its pursuit of cases to discuss the patterns that the students identify as present in the phenomenon. Their data is the set of cases. In essence, the students are analyzing the data to discern the categories that appear among the various aspects of the database thus far accumulated.

The next step is to discern the possible associations between the categories and the outcomes of interest. The class then proceeds with additional cases to consider whether the budding constructs hold in the new situations.

By iterating between the reflective sessions and additional cases, the 'research group' continues to refine the classification schemes and the apparent causal relationships between these aspects of the situations and the desired outcomes. The process is inductive in nature as it moves from observation of the phenomenon through the medium of the cases to the theoretical framework (Christensen and Carlile, 2009, p. 248).

Deductive

A deductive approach is more appropriate when there are already extensively researched theories regarding the phenomenon (Christensen and Carlile, 2009). As an example, the authors use Christensen's teaching of an area in which an initial course design using an inductive process such as described above became what Christensen termed 'an unmitigated disaster' (p. 248). He revised the syllabus so that the students were assigned readings and cases associated with the research discoveries covered in the specific readings.

The students were asked to utilize theory from the assigned readings for analysis and then were asked whether the theoretical constructs adequately explained the phenomenon as described in the assigned case. The students utilized additional sets of readings and cases in subsequent class sessions. With each case the students were expected to utilize their accumulated knowledge to ascertain whether the previous theoretical lenses provide tools to augment the insights that they gleaned:

> The students were expected, at the end of the term, to have acquired knowledge of a set of theories related to the topic and employed them on numerous occasions in the various case settings. During the course of the discussions, discerning students might well note where the theories under consideration did not adequately provide analysis of the situation and guidance for the management. In so doing the expectation was that the student–professor team would continue to refine extant theory through the process.

> The approach is deductive in that it starts with theory, i.e., the general explanation, and moves to the particular, i.e., the case of phenomenon (Christensen and Carlile, 2009, pp. 247–9).

Chapter 6 discusses the abductive approach in comparison with inductive and deductive approaches. The study of the phenomenon in situ with personal observation used, for example, in ethnographic studies, is at this end of the continuum.

At the other end of the continuum are more quantitative approaches that generally use deductive reasoning. This end of the continuum emphasizes data integrity or preciseness of measurement of variables. These designs necessitate larger-scale samples and a more limited set of aspects of the phenomenon (Box 3.1).

Another way to think about our choices of how to study the phenomenon and associated units of analysis is to categorize them on the basis of the number of units and number of time periods we investigate (Table 3.1). In a *speculative* design we study one unit at one point in time or during a specific (usually short) period of time. This research is generally descriptive in nature, but might also be used to compare to a pattern known or expected to

BOX 3.1

THE CONTINUUM OF THEORY DEVELOPMENT-CONFIRMATION/DISCONFIRMATION-TESTING: THE BASICS

Inductive ←————————————————————————→ Deductive

Generally qualitative ←——— Data-gathering methodologies ——→ Generally quantitative

Table 3.1 Basic choices in research designs

		Number of units	
		One	Multiple
Number of time periods	One	1 Speculative	2 Cross-sectional
	Multiple	3 Longitudinal	4 Dynamic

exist. A *cross-sectional* design studies multiple units, each at a point in time. The point in time might be a fairly short period of time such as the formation stage of a new venture or a new group. Our purpose is to make comparisons and develop or confirm/disconfirm existing theory.

A *longitudinal* research involves focusing our attention on the unit or units over time. In longitudinal research we study the same unit over multiple periods. Such a design might study the implementation of a new process in an organization. Or, the design might compare an organization's responses during the recent recession as contrasted to its responses during the ensuing recovery period. Thus the study time period is generally longer. In some studies such as those pursued by business historians the study might span a century or more (e.g., Huber and Van de Ven, 1995)! Or, we can complicate matters by deciding to use a *dynamic* design and study the phenomenon across units with longitudinal data gathered for each unit. These designs are particularly important in studying a process. They attempt to develop the cross-sectional comparisons as well as understand the dynamics of the longitudinal developments. These designs are definitely more complex and consume greater time and resources! An expanded explanation of these four designs appears in in the cells of Appendix Tables 3A.1a and 3A.1b at the end of this chapter.

Another option for research design is what researchers call 'experimental'. In these instances the researcher manipulates the major independent variable under consideration. In an equation the independent variable is the 'X' in the expected causal logic. If the 'X' condition is deliberately manipulated, the design is experimental. If the researcher does not manipulate the condition, the research is essentially observational in nature.

In experimental designs conducted in a behavioral laboratory, the researcher will deliberately interject a change in one or more units after gathering data about the base situation. These studies usually involve a larger-scale sample compared to a case study research design. In an experimental field study the researcher might introduce the change. Another option is to study 'natural experiments' in which the change already exists or is occurring. For example, the researcher might be interested in the differential effects on an organization of an organic or internal growth strategy versus an acquisition strategy. In a case study project, the choice of design might be to compare two companies – one company uses only organic growth and the other has grown through acquisitions. The difficulties of a case study project using a small sample of N = 2 quickly becomes apparent. The organizations may indeed differ. However, the differences may not be attributable to this dichotomy of strategic choices, but instead to other dimensions. We refer to these other dimensions as 'confounding effects' (Schoenherr et al., 2010).

To avoid confounding effects, a skilled researcher will try to hold all aspects of the study constant (*ceteris paribus*). In an N = 2 study, the organizations might come from the same industry, have been started about the same time, be located in a similar region and size of population area, and have similar origins and founding leader profiles. This design is referred to as 'matched pairs'. In matched pairs the researcher is trying to keep as many aspects as possible the same or similar *except* the aspects that are the focus of the study. The emphasis, of course, is on *try* because in practice getting access to the ideal field sites has its own challenges, issues we will address later.[1]

Author Søndergaard's PhD study (1990) is an example of holding things constant in the selection of the unit of analysis in the context of both the organizational unit and the bank practice. In order to obtain interview-based information about delegation in the loan decision-making process, *ceteris paribus* (all other things being equal) was used to isolate the role of differences in national culture on the unit of analysis, i.e., referral to hierarchical higher levels in the loan decision processes. Did values of hierarchical authority influence the involvement of the superior level in the bank? Factors known to influence loan decision-making practices were held constant. For instance, the branches were matched, that is, branches had to have the following characteristics: (1) same mix of private and business customers, (2) about equal size in terms of individuals employed, and (3) similar levels of turnover or revenues generated. The banks were asked to suggest a competent entrusted banker in a branch to participate in the interview. There were two main bank examples in France and Denmark. The Danish main example of these was situated in Vesterbro, Copenhagen. The French main example was a branch situated in Clichy, Paris. The branches belonged to banks with nationwide banks (Søndergaard, 1990, pp. 199–222). The interviews focused on how the interviewee, the banker, would make a decision about a fictional loan application. The loan application came from a trusted customer who needed immediate approval for a loan that exceeded the authority of the interviewed banker. The banker's direct superiors were not to be included in the decision in any way (Søndergaard, 1990, p. 176).[2] What was interesting was to develop an understanding of the decisions and the rationale that the French and Danish bank interviewees provided.

Generally, small sample sizes are not used for case study situations where the researcher is manipulating conditions. However, author Søndergaard's study ultimately included a large sample of interviewees in branches of three different banks in both France and Denmark located outside of the capitals with a total of 60 persons interviewed and compared with the findings from the two main examples (Søndergaard, 1990, p. 143). Exceptions include very early stages of medical research where the effects of the substance being studied may be used in a small number of individuals as a treatment of last resort for very ill patients where all other known interventions have been exhausted. In these instances using individuals for a control group in which no treatment or a placebo are given may not be ethically appropriate. However, there are also ethical issues of administering the treatment since the negative effects of the substance on the individuals are unknown. The choice of methodology involves, among other issues, making tradeoffs between data integrity or internal validity and currency or external validity as mentioned in Chapter 2. That choice very much depends on the theoretical development to date as represented in the research literature regarding the phenomenon, the purpose of the research, and the nature of the phenomenon.[3]

A final word concerns case study method in combination with other methodologies. One combination is a case study or set of case studies followed by a qualitative study utilizing structured interviews or a written survey.[4] Another combination is a case study followed by a quantitative study such as a questionnaire survey.

3.3 How does the state of the literature impact on our choice?

Considering the state of the literature is an important issue. Where there is very little prior research and theory, a case can be used to begin to develop theory. Using an inductive process the researcher can begin to discern possible relationships between aspects of the case study data. The addition of other case studies can augment understanding of the phenomenon. The researcher can proceed with additional cases to consider whether the budding constructs hold in new situations. By iterating between reflection and data from additional cases, the researcher can continue to refine the classification schemes and the apparent causal relationships between these aspects of the situations and desired outcomes. This process is inductive in nature because it moves from observation of the phenomenon through the medium of the cases to the theoretical framework (Christensen and Carlile, 2009, p. 248).

A deductive process, on the other hand, is more appropriate when the phenomenon has been extensively researched and there are already theories regarding that phenomenon. In these instances the researcher utilizes existing theory for analysis of the data and then asks whether the theoretical constructs adequately explain the phenomenon. Deductive approaches generally characterize studies that rely on larger-scale samples and quantifiable data that permits testing of hypotheses developed from existing theory. The basic relationship between inductive and deductive reasoning is depicted in Box 3.1. In Chapter 6 we will look at inductive and deductive reasoning processes briefly again as we consider abductive reasoning, a third reasoning process. Other aspects of the research process as related to research choices are depicted in Box 3.2.

A critical point is that the research process be as transparent as possible.[5] Thus, it is important, within the limitations of space imposed by the professor's instructions or those of the publication outlet, to describe the research process as fully as possible. In addition, the researcher must describe the data and how the data and data analysis support the conclusions, however tentative. To this end Lillis (2002) and Lillis and Mundy (2005) build on the well-known advice for qualitative research from Miles and Huberman (1994) by invoking the accounting notion of an 'audit trail'. The audit trail incorporates keeping track of sources of data, analysis of data, and the connections between the data and the development of theory and constructs – no trivial task.

BOX 3.2

THE CONTINUUM OF THEORY DEVELOPMENT-CONFIRMATION/ DISCONFIRMATION-TESTING AND RELATED ISSUES

Inductive → Deductive

Generally qualitative → Generally quantitative

Data-gathering methodologies ←→

Theory confirmation/disconfirmation ←→

Theory generation

Little theory exists

Unstructured interviews and observations

Perry: "focuses on the deep structure of *rich descriptions* of the context within which social events occur. Indeed, they think that case studies should be mere studies and not have any theorizing associated with them. Also at the extreme left-hand point, grounded theory develops a theory from the data alone, without any reference to prior theory" (Perry, 2001, p.308, original emphasis; see also Dyer, Wilkins, and Eisenhardt, 1991).

Theory confirmation/disconfirmation

Some theory exists

Structured interviews and observation protocols

Perry: 'describes a very flexible process that has inductive features such as "flexible and opportunistic data collection methods" that allow additions to questions in an interviewer's guide during a series of interviews. Moreover, she (Eisenhardt, 1989) even thinks that the initial research problem, "may shift during the research" as data is gathered, and "research is begun as close as possible to the inductive ideal of *no theory* under consideration and no hypothesis to test"' (Perry, 2001, p.308, original emphasis; see also Eisenhardt, 1989).

Perry: 'Yin (1993, p.xvi) is closer to the middle, theory confirming and/or disconfirming, *deduction end* of the induction–deduction continuum. He has a very tight structure set up *before interviews* are begun, with "the posing of clear [and precise] questions. . .[and] the use of theory and reviews of previous research to develop hypothesis and rival hypothesis" . He is explicit in arguing against changes in direction after the research has begun and for a standard consistent interviewer's guide used in *all* interviews (Yin, 1994). That is, Yin argues for the middle, confirmatory/disconfirmatory stage' (Perry, 2001, p.309, original emphasis).

Theory testing

Theory is well developed

Well established premises

Perry does not discuss this end of the continuum. However, at this end of the continuum we are usually dealing with well-developed theories that the researcher is interested in replicating or testing in a different setting than has previously been used or in extending the theory by adding additional variables.

Such approaches generally involve larger-scale samples and quantified or quantifiable data that are subjected to parametric statistical tests. Such tests generally assume the data approximates a normal distribution.

Source: Adapted and augmented from Perry (2001).

Another important issue is that the researcher should be very clear about the generalizability of the findings. Christensen and Carlile argue that '[g]eneralizability comes with prescriptive theory' (2009, p. 244). They cite Yin, who states that 'case studies, like experiments, are generalizable to theoretical propositions' (1994, p. 21). Christensen and Carlile then move forward to argue: 'In the descriptive stage [propositions] are not, and need not be, generalizable to the populations or universes in which those situations are nested. Generalizability comes with prescriptive theory' (2009, p. 244).

We do NOT concur that generalizability necessarily accompanies prescriptive theory, although generalizability is a purpose of prescriptive theory. Prescriptive theory, after all, aims to suggest what the unit of analysis (e.g., an organization) should do under certain contingent conditions. However, prescriptive theory emanating from case research results might be severely limited in its generalizability.

We do concur that findings do not necessarily have to be generalizable as long as the researcher makes the point clear. The important issue is that the more generalizable the findings the more useful the work is in helping us to understand, predict, and control our world! Our underlying premise is that in improving control we are designing and implementing an improved future for a broader set of players in our shared social system.

3.4   When is case research *not* case research?

Another way of asking this question is: how many cases are included in a research program or project before it is *not* 'case research'? The short answer is that there is no definitive number. In some sense, all research is case research since each investigational unit is a case. Where we draw the line in terms of how large the sample size or N can be before a research investigation is not case research is certainly one issue some would like to 'discuss'. However, one fact is certainly uncontroversial – the more cases involved in an investigation the less investigatory time can be spent on each case. Thus, as the size of the sample goes up, there is less and less opportunity to develop what Geertz (1973), Eisenhardt (1989), and others refer to as 'thick description'.

Standard statistical theory has suggestions with regard to how many cases are appropriate. Smaller sample sizes can often use non-parametric statistics, such as chi square, as a means of ascertaining, for example, whether there are significant differences between different groupings, units of analysis, or groups of subjects within a case. Many statistical techniques, especially those that are parametric in nature, simply are not applicable in smaller size samples that characterize case study research methodology.

3.5 Which is better – qualitative data or quantitative data?

One significant controversy regarding reliability of data is whether qualitative or quantitative data is more trustworthy. Those embracing the positivistic traditions typically argue that quantitative data is more objective. Let us examine that argument more carefully. Quantitative data in the management fields is often in the form of measures such as Likert-scale responses from surveys.[6] Concerns about the objectivity of the researcher in designing the questions and overall survey have long been debated.

Financial measures are often regarded as 'hard data'. However, financial data are replete with difficulties throughout the entire process of ascertaining 'the number' to record. As one example of issues related to financial data, electric power company accounting personnel regularly use personal judgments in recording an expenditure as an expense of the period or as a capital expenditure. The former reduces the net income or surplus for the period. The latter increases the asset base and only reduces the net income in subsequent periods as it is depreciated under whatever depreciation rules apply at the time of the expenditure.

In another example, Taylor (1988) found in her research that the estimated expense levels of a division can shift dramatically depending on the role the head of the division is playing at the time. The profit picture may be presented very positively if the head of a division is reviewing a unit's performance with superiors when the division head's yearly bonus is dependent on the profitability of the unit. The financial picture may be presented quite differently when the division head is a potential buyer of a unit to be sold, especially a unit that has not had much interest from external buyers.

The sometimes arrogance of those who rely on 'hard numbers' reveals a woeful ignorance of the processes of decision, negotiation, and personal behaviors in the chains of events that lead to the audited data that a public company presents to its shareholders and the world, or a private company to its owners.[7] We revisit this set of issues of the controversy between the 'hard' and 'soft' scientists in Chapter 6.

The subjectivity of data in qualitative studies may be more obvious. For example, in ethnographic studies the researcher uses observations and participant observation where either the researcher is tired or personally upset may influence the recording of the data. But, as Christensen and Carlile put it so aptly:

> There should be no smugness among quantitative researchers about the alleged objectivity of their data, and no defensiveness among field researchers about the subjectivity of theirs. We are all in the same subjective boat, and are obligated to do our best to be humble and honest with ourselves and our colleagues about where our data come from as we participate individually within and collectively across the theory-building cycle (Christensen and Carlile, 2009, p. 243).

As researchers we have fiduciary responsibilities to our subjects, to the phenomenon, to our profession, to practitioners, and to the broader public to be as objective as possible in garnering, analyzing, and interpreting our data. Ours is a heavy burden to validly reflect current practice and potentially improve practice as well.

3.6　What is the 'right' research design?

The short answer is that there is no one 'right' design. The choice depends on multiple factors. In this book we are focusing on case research methodology. This approach fits better in some situations than in others. If the literature, for example, is well developed with robust models, case research methodology may not be at all appropriate – unless we find that the pursuit of an outlier may be of importance or the context of the phenomenon has so significantly shifted since the development of the original models that the phenomenon needs to be approached anew.

Sometimes the setting itself does not lend itself to a positivistic approach. An example is the application that Anyansi-Archibong (1985) made of Chandler's thesis to Nigeria, a developing country. Prior to the time of her study, Chandler's model of 'structure follows strategy' (Chandler, 1962) had been applied in the developed countries including the United States and several European countries. It might have appeared that the situation was ripe for a deductive approach using theory testing. However, the data regarding Nigerian businesses was, at best, fragmentary. In addition, the choice of a questionnaire study would have been fraught with mistrust that was rampant between the multiple tribes that made up the country. The mistrust was a barrier that personal presence could potentially overcome. Further, Anyansi-Archibong wanted to study the process of the interactivity of the evolution of strategy and structures. She wanted to focus on the 'hows' and 'whys'. Thus, she chose a robust case research approach with fruitful results.[8]

Instead of choosing a theory-testing approach (see Box 3.2) Anyansi-Archibong chose a hybrid of matching her data to the components of the Chandlerian model (see Anyansi-Archibong, Taylor, and Coates, 2010) to ascertain whether the model did indeed hold in the Nigerian setting. Given her sample size of nine organizations, she could not make assertions with the probabilistic results that might have emanated from a larger-scale study. However, she could and did propose modifications to Chandler's thesis. Her research is best described as conducted in theory confirmation mode.

Could Anyansi-Archibong have chosen a different approach? Perhaps. But in a developing nation where the understanding of the evolutionary process was her purpose, her choice of case study was appropriate. And, in the end, perhaps as with all research, two issues were important. What would the supervising committee of her dissertation research approve and would the results be acceptable to a broader scholarly audience? Anyansi-Archibong did not regret her decision. The research led to several publications. The choice was also fruitful long term in terms of the relationships she developed for future research.

Why then undertake a qualitative/ethnographic approach to our research, such as a case study approach? A major answer is that we elect case study methodology because human researchers have a greater ability to see complex relationships among data and to interpret the results in terms of their relevance for practice than mechanical processes have demonstrated. As one researcher urged, case researchers should emphasize the strengths of case research:

> [. . .]in adding to more conventional approaches. . .These strengths include the telling of convincing stories and the ability to express the uncertainty and undecidability of organizational life (Kelemen and Rumens, 2008). These are rare qualities, which give case researchers a distinct position in contributing to the appreciation of the complexity of organizational action (De Loo and Lowe, 2012, p. 5).

3.7   Concluding thoughts

In this chapter we examined the iterative nature of the stages of the research process. We did so to remind us that although we might depict the research process as a series of linear steps, it is really an interactive phenomenon. The iterative nature of the process is especially relevant to case study research. The process might evolve as you become acquainted with the site or subject first-hand and as you glean greater insights and find the need to revise initial ideas.

The chapter has looked at the varieties of research design. Our simplification considered that case study research design essentially took into account two major factors – whether we study one or multiple cases and what number of time periods we target to gather data about each case.

Further, we understand that the state of the literature impacts on our choice of design. If few have studied the phenomenon, our research is likely to be exploratory. Exploratory research requires intimacy with the subject and the number of cases is likely to be small, perhaps only one. If the state of the research topic is considerably advanced, we are more likely to want to delve into more instances of a narrow band of the phenomenon. Case research, generally but not always, is used as earlier stage research where the theory is not well developed.

Case research is more likely to utilize an inductive reasoning process. Our data is more likely to be more qualitative in nature. But quantitative data about our subjects or sites might well be appropriate depending on the nature of our research questions, the data available, or the data we can acquire. The controversies regarding whether quantitative data is superior to qualitative observations may never be resolved, but we draw attention to issues related to quantitative measures as well as qualitative observations. There is no exact number of cases that determines whether a study is a case study project just as there is no one right research design.

Overall, it is important that the research design we choose fits with the issues we have discussed in the previous chapter – our motivation, the research purpose, the questions we have formed, and the unit of analysis we have chosen, as well as the other factors we have discussed in this chapter. Above all, as we emphasize several times in this book, all of what we do must be as transparent as possible to those who may read reports or articles about our work and especially for those who follow in our footsteps.

? END OF CHAPTER QUESTIONS AND ANSWERS

1 **What are the stages in the research design process?** The stages in the research design process are (1) motivation, objective, questions, unit (MPQU); (2) state of the literature; and (3) research design.
2 **What options for research design are available for case study methodology?** An inductive

approach is associated with generally qualitative data-gathering methodologies. A deductive approach is generally linked with quantitative data-gathering methodologies.

3 **How does the state of the literature impact on our choice?** The state of the literature impacts the choice of design. An exploratory research design is likely if few have studied the phenomenon. If the state of the research topic is considerably advanced, we are more likely to want to delve into more instances of a narrow band of the phenomenon. Generally, case research designs are selected as an earlier stage of research, where the theory is not well developed.

4 **When is case research *not* case research?** There is no definitive number for how many cases to include in the research project before it is *not* 'case research'. The more cases that are included in the study the less investigatory time can be spent on each case.

5 **Which is better – qualitative data or quantitative data?** The question reflects a long-standing controversy regarding reliability of data – whether qualitative or quantitative data is more trustworthy. The answer depends on the research purpose and on the research traditions and skills of the researcher. Researchers following positivistic traditions argue that quantitative data is more objective. Researchers following interpretivist traditions argue that qualitative data is more credible. Both types of data are related to/rooted in subjectivity. Both types of data call for the researcher to be humble and honest about where the data come from and to be as objective as possible when gathering, analyzing and interpreting the data.

6 **What is the 'right' research design?** There is no *one* 'right' design. There is an appropriate research design depending on research purpose. The research design should fit the purpose.

NOTES

1 See discussions in Gerring and McDermott (2007) and their references to Campbell (1968 [1988]) and Shadish, Cook, and Campbell (2002). Gerring and McDermott note: 'Ceteris paribus [sic] assumptions are considerably more difficult to achieve in observational settings. . .the point remains that they *can* be achieved in observational settings, just as they can be violated in experimental settings. As J.F. Mill observes, "we may either *find* an instance in nature suited to our purposes, or by an artificial arrangement of circumstances, *make* one. The value of the instances depends on what it is in itself, not the mode in which it is obtained. . . There is in short, no difference in kind, no real logical distinctions between the two processes of investigation" (1832 and 1872, p. 249 [original emphasis]). It is the satisfaction of ceteris paribus [sic] assumptions, not the use of a manipulated treatment or a randomized control group that qualifies a research product as methodologically sound' (Gerring and McDermott, 2007, p. 692).

2 The real-life cases were not reported anywhere, but they did help the researcher ascertain that the fictional situation was close to reality so that the results could be judged valid from the perspective of practitioners.

3 As Bonoma (1985) put it: 'Case research, as the term is used here, refers to the qualitative and field-based construction of case studies. It is guided by a process model of discovery which leads to 1) a set of theoretical generalizations from the clinical observations, 2) clinical "constraint testing" of these generalizations, and eventually 3) a clinically validated theory of some marketing phenomenon' (p. 199).

4 Two excellent examples of multiple-stage dissertations are Coates (2004) and Puia (*1993*).

5 See Dubois and Gibbert (2010).

6 Survey research is extensively used in many fields such as organizational behavior, marketing, strategic management, and branches of sociology. There is extensive literature that deals with issues such as phrasing of questions and number of numerical points to present. There are excellent researchers whose skill in the survey method and objectivity in applying the method is unquestionable. However, the objectivity of the respondent *is* questionable. How the respondent views the survey, and interprets the questions, may be a function of how she or he responds while fatigued or well-rested, angry or calm, sad or happy, hungry or sleepy from a big meal, not to mention ethnic and geographic influences on interpretation of words and phrasing.

7 Christensen and Carlile (2009) cite Johnson and Kaplan (1987) as demonstrating 'quite convincingly that

the numbers representing revenues, costs, and profits in financial statements are the result of processes of estimation, negotiation, debate, and politics that can produce grossly inaccurate reflections of true cost and profit' (Christensen and Carlile, 2009, p. 243).

8   Anyansi-Archibong (1985), revised, was published as *Strategy and Structure of Enterprise in a Developing Country* in 1988. See also Anyansi-Archibong (1995) and Anyansi-Archibong, Taylor, and Coates (2010).

REFERENCES

Aaboen, L., A. Dubois, and F. Lind (2012), 'Processes in longitudinal multiple case studies', *Industrial Marketing Management*, **41**(2), 235–46.

Åkesson, M. and P. Skålén (2011), 'Towards a service-dominant professional identity', *Journal of Service Management*, **22**(1), 23–38.

Anyansi-Archibong, C.B. (1985), 'Evolution of firms: Strategy and structure of enterprise in a third world country', dissertation, University of Kansas.

Anyansi-Archibong, C.B. (1988), *Strategy and Structure of Enterprise in a Developing Country*, Aldershot, UK: Avebury.

Anyansi-Archibong, C.B. (1995), *Planning in Developing Countries: A Strategic Assessment*, Chicago, IL: The Planning Forum.

Anyansi-Archibong, C., M.L. Taylor, and T.L. Coates (2010), 'Reflections on Alfred D. Chandler, Jr., Evolution of firms: Strategy and structure of enterprise in a developing country', *Journal of Applied Management and Entrepreneurship*, **15**(1), 96–114.

Bonoma, T.V. (1985), 'Case research in marketing: Opportunities, problems, and a process', *Journal of Marketing Research*, **22**(2), 199–208.

Campbell, D.T. (1968 [1988]). 'The Connecticut crackdown on speeding: Time-series data in quasi-experimental analysis', in E.S. Overman (ed.), *Methodology and Epistemology for Social Science*, Chicago, IL: University of Chicago Press, pp. 222–38.

Chandler, A.D. (1962), *Strategy and Structure*, Cambridge, MA: MIT Press.

Christensen, C.L. and P.R. Carlile (2009), 'Course research: Using case method to build and teach management theory', *Academy of Management Learning & Education*, **8**(2), 240–51.

Coates, T. (2004), 'The development of core competence through emerging technology innovation: An empirical investigation', dissertation, Rensselaer Polytechnic Institute.

De Loo, I. and A. Lowe (2012), 'Authoritative interpretation in understanding accounting practice through case research', *Management Accounting Research*, **23**(1), 3–16.

Dubois, A. and M. Gibbert (2010), 'From complexity to transparency: Managing the interplay between theory, method and empirical phenomena in IMM case studies', *Industrial Marketing Management*, **39**(1), 553–60.

Dyer, W.G., Jr., A.L. Wilkins, and K.L. Eisenhardt (1991), 'Better stories, not better constructs, to generate better theories: A rejoinder to Eisenhardt', *Academy of Management Review*, **16**(3), 613–19.

Eisenhardt, K.M. (1989), 'Building theories from case study research', *The Academy of Management Review*, **14**(4), 532–50.

Foscht, T., B. Swoboda, and D. Morschett (2006), 'Electronic commerce-based internationalisation of small, niche-oriented retailing companies: The case of Blue Tomato and the snowboard industry', *International Journal of Retail & Distribution Management*, **34**(7), 556–72.

Geertz, C. (1973), *Interpretation of Cultures*, New York: Basic Books.

Gerring, J. (2004), 'What is a case study and what is it good for?' *The American Political Science Review*, **98**(2), 341–54.

Gerring, J. and R. McDermott (2007), 'An experimental template for case study research', *American Journal of Political Science*, **51**(3), 688–701.

Hiebl, M.R.W. and B. Feldbauer-Durstmüller (2014), 'What can the corporate world learn from the cellarer?: Examining the role of a Benedictine abbey's CFO', *Society and Business Review*, **9**(1), 51–73.

Huber, G.P. and A.H. Van de Ven (eds) (1995), *Longitudinal Field Research Methods, Studying Process Patterns of Organizational Change*, Thousand Oaks, CA: Sage.

Jaatinen, M. and R. Lavikka (2008), 'Common understanding as a basis for coordination', *Corporate Communications*, **13**(2), 147–67.

Jarvinen, J. (2006), 'Institutional pressures for adopting new cost accounting systems in Finnish hospitals: Two longitudinal case studies', *Financial Accountability & Management*, **22**(1), 21–46.

Johnson, H.T. and R. Kaplan (1987), *Relevance Lost*, Boston, MA: Harvard Business School Press.

Keating, P.J. (1995), 'A framework for classifying and evaluating the theoretical contributions of case research in management accounting', *Journal of Management Accounting Research*, **7**(1), 66–86.

Kelemen, M. and N. Rumens (2008), *An Introduction to Critical Management Research*, Los Angeles, CA: Sage.

Lillis, A.M. (2002), 'Managing multiple dimensions of manufacturing performance – an exploratory study', *Accounting, Organizations and Society*, **27**(6), 497–529.

Lillis, A.M and J. Mundy (2005), 'Cross-sectional field studies in management accounting research – closing the gaps between surveys and case studies', *Journal of Management Accounting Research*, **17**(1), 119–41.

Lundervold, D.A. and M.F. Belwood (2000), 'The best kept secret in counseling: Single-case (N-1) experimental designs', *Journal of Counseling and Development*, **78**(1), 92–102.

Miles, M.B. and A.B. Huberman (1994), *Qualitative Data Analysis: An Expanded Sourcebook* (2nd edition), Thousand Oaks, CA: Sage.

Millward, H. and A. Lewis (2005), 'Barriers to successful new product development within small manufacturing companies', *Journal of Small Business and Enterprise Development*, **12**(3), 379–94.

Nordman, E.R. and S. Melen (2008), 'The impact of different kinds of knowledge for the internationalization process of born globals in the biotech business', *Journal of World Business*, **43**(2), 171–85.

Perry, C. (2001), 'Case research in marketing', *The Marketing Review*, **1**(3), 303–23.

Puia, G.M. (1993), 'The effects of corporate restructuring on the adoption of innovations: An analysis of division-level management buyouts', dissertation, University of Kansas.

Schoenherr, T., D. Hilpert, A.K. Soni, M.A. Venkataramanan, and V.A. Mabert (2010), 'Enterprise systems complexity and its antecedents: A grounded-theory approach', *International Journal of Operations & Production Management*, **30**(6), 639–68.

Shadish, W.R., T.D. Cook, and D.T. Campbell (2002), *Experimental and Quasi-experimental Designs for Generalized Causal Inference*, Boston, MA: Houghton Mifflin.

Søndergaard, M. (1990), 'På sporet af den nationale kulturs konsekvenser. En sammenligning af praksis i danske og franske pengeinstitutter, den nationale kulturs betydning' [In search of national cultures' consequences. A comparison of practices in Danish and French banks, the significance of national culture], PhD dissertation, Aarhus Business School.

Taylor, M. (1988), *Divesting Business Units – Making the Decision and Making it Work*, Lexington, MA: Lexington Books.

Wantchekon, L. (2003), 'Clientelism and voting behavior: Evidence from a field experiment in Benin', *World Politics*, **55**(3), 399–422.

Yin, R.K. (1993), *Applications of Case Study Research, Applied Social Research Methods, Vol. 34*, Newbury Park, CA: Sage.

Yin, R.K. (1994), *Case Study Research: Designs and Methods*, 2nd edition, Thousand Oaks, CA: Sage.

Yin, R.K. (2003). *Case Study Research: Design and Methods*, 3rd edition, Thousand Oaks, CA: Sage.

Yuko, M., L.M. Visconti, and P. Maclaran (2012), 'Researchers' introspection for multi-sited ethnographers: A xenoheteroglossic autoethnography', *Journal of Business Research*, **65**(4), 483–9.

Appendix

Table 3A.1a Comparing characteristics of the basic choices in research designs – speculative and cross-unit[a]

	Number of units	
	One	Multiple
No. of time periods: one	1 **Speculative:** This research approach yields a description of a situation. The researcher or informants might additionally use argument or logic to speculate on what *might* happen if aspects of the situation are different or certain changes were made. Modeling provides a similar logic, and in some instances it might be possible to propose a tentative model or compare the experience in the unit of analysis to an existing model. However, finding a published case study that focuses on one unit of analysis in one time period is infrequent. Consulting projects might use this design. For research purposes there are significant limitations on generalizing from one unit of analysis at one point in time[b] One example is a study that examined the role of the cellarer in the order of monks called the Rule of St. Benedictine. The purpose of the study was to understand that role and what aspects might be transferred to the role of the CFO in modern corporations. From their observations the authors speculated regarding transferability (Hiebl and Feldbauer-Durstmüller, 2014)	2 **Cross-unit:** If the researcher has access to multiple units of analysis (e.g., organizations, groups, or individuals), a cross-sectional design is possible[c] Nordman and Melen (2008) chose multiple case studies within the same industrial context. They did so to 'facilitate comparison through replication of results, either literally (when similar results emerge) or theoretically (when contrary results emerge for predictable reasons) and, thus, enable analytical generalization' (p. 178). These two authors noted that '[c]ase studies rely on analytical generalization, in which the investigator strives to make a generalization about a particular set of results so as to fit it into a broader theory. To strengthen the external validity of our multiple case studies, we followed an experimental replication-like logic when collecting the data (Yin, 2003). To insure that the same topics were covered in all the firms, we utilized a three-and-a-half page interview guide' (2008, p. 178)

Notes:
a   See also Gerring (2004, p. 343) who uses the terms 'Temporal variation' (No/Yes) and 'Spatial variation' (No/Yes) for the two axes.
b   See Gerring and McDermott (2007) who use the term 'Counterfactual comparison' for cell 1, which we have here labeled as 'Speculative', meaning through argument or logic either the researcher or the informants would contemplate what *might* happen. Modeling provides a similar logic. In this article Gerring and McDermott use the terms 'Temporal variation' and 'Spatial variation' for the axes (see Gerring and McDermott,2007, esp. p. 690). On the other hand, what Yin (2003) calls 'embedded, single-case design' avoids confounding effects that can emanate when a researcher chooses a multi-site or -subject design. Findings may be robust as applied to the setting, but the generalizability to other settings has to be based on analytical rather statistical analysis (see Åkesson and Skålén, 2011) and thus speculative, hence the use of that word to designate this cell (Keating, 1995). The strength of the single case is that it eliminates confounding effects of interfirm research. The strength of the embedded design is that it yields a large sample of data that can be subjected to statistical test. The results of embedded, single-case studies may be not strictly generalizable, but they do render a rich and broadly applicable body of evidence.
c   Multiple-site ethnographic studies are increasingly used in marketing research. Yuko and Maclaran (2012) detail a multiple case study that involved multiple countries.

Table 3A.1b Comparing characteristics of the basic choices in research designs – longitudinal and dynamic

	Number of units	
	One	Multiple
Number of time periods: multiple	3 **Longitudinal:** Sometimes having a control group is not possible or ethically feasible. Studying one unit over a sufficiently elongated time period in which a change has taken place from one time period to the other might make observations possible. For example, Foscht, Swoboda, and Morschett (2006) were interested in the 'born global' phenomenon. These researchers studied the Blue Tomato, the online snowboard retailer founded by a champion snowboarder. The authors followed the company over approximately a decade. They demonstrated the differences between this 'born global' phenomenon and how it evolved as contrasted to the phases of the evolution of internationalized firms that were depicted in the literature[a] In counseling psychology the emphasis has been on group experimental designs and the statistical analyses that are necessarily related. But, as Lundervold and Belwood (2000, n.p.) point out, these approaches 'are not directly relevant to everyday practice' primarily because 'group research design is seldom possible in clinical settings for a number of reasons, including the fact that most counselors frequently work with one individual at a time'. Counselors work with their clients over extended periods of time and use the changes associated with client adoption of the counselor's recommendations as evidence of how effective the treatment has been	4 **Dynamic:** In each of the two instances below the researchers chose to study multiple organizations over time in order to understand how aspects of the organization evolved One of the studies used in-depth interviews in three dynamic start-up Scandinavian companies to determine how the firms developed their first customers. The research team used a 'snowball' technique to identify the additional firms beyond the first company. The semi-structured interview guide focused on how the customer relationships initiated and developed. The researchers used the 200 pages of interview transcripts for their analysis and then utilized network drawings to show (a) initial relationships, (b) current relationships, and (c) anticipated future relationships. Other than their startup status the research team did not attempt to match the firms as the focus was on relationship or network building processes (Aaboen, Dubois, and Lind, 2012) In still another approach the researcher used (a) archival data and personal involvement observations over more than five years for the first case and (b) for the second case the data source was a research diary, which a member of the organization kept for one-and-a-half years. The focus of the study was the implementation of activity-based costing (ABC) systems in two Finnish hospitals. In this study the researcher chose two hospitals that performed a similar set of functions. The purpose of the study was to understand how the systems and motivation to implement changed over time (Jarvinen, 2006)[b]

Notes:
a   See also Millward and Lewis (2005).
b   In a third example, with a sample size of nine, the political scientist chose to examine the differential effects of different ways of marketing candidates. Within each of eight electoral districts, the researcher chose three villages (24 villages in all). Each of the villages can be considered a case study. In one of the three villages the marketing approach focused on appeals to the client's concerns. In the second village marketing efforts focused on national programs. In the third village both types of appeals were used. In all eight electoral districts the villages in which the candidates used client-oriented appeals were more successful in terms of votes for the candidate (Wantchekon, 2003). Also see Aaboen, Dubois, and Lind (2012). Another interesting design is Jaatinen and Lavikka (2008).

Table 3A.2a Comparing hypothesis testing, hypothesis generation, and case research –
purpose, usual methodologies, and data-gathering techniques

	Hypothesis testing	Hypothesis generation	Case research
Purpose	Must use sufficient sized sample to demonstrate whether the tendencies suggested in the hypotheses hold within the sample of the selected population	Establishment from the data itself of possible hypotheses to be tested with another set of data	Tendency may be either hypothesis generating or hypothesis testing
Usual methodologies	Empirical (which means based on data) 'quantitative' data, which includes data that can be quantified from a sample of sufficient size to permit statistical testing of the hypotheses	Empirical (which means based on data) 'qualitative' data with which statistical testing usually does not play as large a role, but may use non-parametric tests. Tests may be based on qualitative logic. Emphasis is on developing a holistic understanding of the subject or subjects	Empirical (which means based on data) 'qualitative' data use in which statistical testing usually does not play a role; tests generally based on qualitative logic
Data-gathering techniques	Typically includes: secondary databases; observations; survey instruments; structured interviews; participant observation used only if observations can be measured	Typically includes: interviews: structured or unstructured; participant observation (such as that used in ethnographic oriented research)	Typically more qualitative, prior reading on the issues and subject organization if such documentation on the subject is available. Use of internal documentation and interviews, often, but not always unstructured (primary data)

Table 3A.2b Comparing hypothesis testing, hypothesis generation, and case research –
displayed knowledge, unit of analysis, and role of gatekeeper

	Hypothesis testing	Hypothesis generation	Case research
Displayed knowledge of the phenomenon in the existing literature regarding the research issues/foci	Note that researchers should be familiar with prior research involving the same issues (and kinds of subjects) as the assumption is that there is sufficient extant knowledge to generate testable hypotheses or to test hypotheses that have been suggested in prior publications	Researchers should be familiar with prior research involving the same issues (and kinds of subjects). If the sample is small, the researcher can and should be held more responsible for a more holistic understanding of each subject. For example, if a subject is an organization, the researcher might be held responsible for reading the extant literature on the organization	The case researcher's acquaintance with the literature regarding the case issue is displayed in the accompanying Instructor's Manual[a] Increasingly *Case Research Journal* reviewers are requiring the case researchers to demonstrate greater knowledge of the literature regarding the issues/phenomena that the case deals with. Typically the reviewer's comment will be something like 'Insufficient link to theory'. This evaluation essentially means that the case researcher has not compared the information in the case to see if it supports or denies existing theory. Note that one of the shortcomings of teaching case research is that the case researchers are not held responsible for examining existing case research databases to identify (and read!) prior cases regarding the same organization
Unit of analysis	Varies from individual (or smaller sub-system) to organization to interorganizational to nation and beyond	Same	Same
Role of gatekeeper	Varies with a number of variables including relationships between the researcher and gatekeeper, the expertise level of the gatekeeper in the issues and the purpose of the research	Tends to be more intimate, if only because sample is smaller and the researcher can maintain a relationship with the smaller set of individuals	Tends to be more intimate, if only because sample is smaller and the researcher can maintain a relationship with the smaller set of individuals

Note: a. The Instructor's Manual is variously referred to as a 'Teaching Note' or 'Analytic Note'.

Table 3A.2c Comparing hypothesis testing, hypothesis generation, and case research – sources of bias

	Hypothesis testing	Hypothesis generation	Case research
Sources of bias	Biases occur in early choices regarding such decisions as the unit of analysis, boundaries of the issue domain(s), population/sample May occur in choices of coding, consolidation of data points, choice of statistical tests, and interpretations Runs the risk if data is from one organization of being suppressed if the organization can be identified or gatekeepers take umbrage at the outcomes	Biases occur in early choices such as unit of analysis, boundaries of the issue domain(s), population/sample May occur in choices of data to include as illustrative of the themes, describing the characteristics such as organizational culture and leadership	Biases occur in early choices such as unit of analysis, boundaries of the issue domain(s), population/sample May occur in choices of data to include as illustrative of the themes, describing the characteristics such as organizational culture and leadership

4

Managing research sites, data, and information sources challenges

'Data! Data! Data!' he cried impatiently. 'I can't make bricks without clay'.
(Sherlock Holmes, *The Adventure of the Copper Beeches*)

LEARNING OBJECTIVES

This chapter responds to the following questions:

1 What are the differences between primary and secondary data?

2 What issues arise in site selection, entry, maintenance, and exit processes?

3 What special considerations are important for interviews, participant observation, and documentation?

How does Sherlock choose his 'sites' or cases from where the data come? One hint is in *Copper Beeches* as the scenario below suggests. Sherlock and his ever-faithful friend Dr. Watson were travelling through what appeared to be peaceful countryside when Watson cried, 'Good heavens! Who would associate crime with these dear old [country] homesteads?'. To which Sherlock replied:

> They always fill me with a certain horror. It is my belief, Watson, founded upon my experience, that the lowest and vilest alleys in London do not present a more dreadful record of sin than does the smiling and beautiful countryside. . .the reason [for this phenomenon] is very obvious. The pressure of public opinion can do in the town what the law cannot accomplish. There is no lane so vile that the scream of a tortured child, or the thud of a drunkard's blow, does not beget sympathy and indignation among the neighbours, and then the whole machinery of justice is ever so close that a word of complaint can set it going, and there is but a step between

the crime and the dock. But look at these lonely houses, each in its own fields, filled for the most part with poor ignorant folk who know little of the law. Think of the deeds of hellish cruelty, the hidden wickedness which may go on, year in, year out, in such places, and none the wiser.

Clearly Sherlock chose, as he put it, 'Interesting cases only please', which, in his experience, the countryside could yield – hence, the preference of this pre-eminent 'researcher'.

In Chapter 2 we examined interactions among four issues – our own motivations for undertaking the research, the purpose of the research, the research questions that emanate from that purpose, and the unit of analysis. Guidance from Chapter 3 has led to at least a preliminary design. Our next challenges are identification of sites or subjects and the gathering of data. We have to approach the sites or subjects and convince them to participate in our research. Cultivation of the relationships, management of the access, maintenance of the relationships, and ultimately exit, are all processes we must manage. Simultaneously, we need to identify the potential sources of data that we will need and determine how to gather the data we need. Analyzing the data is interactive with the kinds of questions we are asking and the kind of data our research design requires. The challenges of analysis follow on the heels of research site and data source identification – but we will leave that set of issues as the topic of Chapter 5!

In the course of our discussion we will provide examples and caveats from the work of colleagues from various fields as well as from our own work. The reciprocal relationships between study purpose and design on the one hand and the issues we cover in this chapter on the other, are summarized in Figure 4.1.

4.1   What are the differences between primary and secondary data?

Whether we need mostly primary or secondary data to accomplish our research goals influences the degree of access that we need to subjects or sites. Primary data refers to data supplied directly from the site (or subject) to the researcher. Generally, primary data requires greater access to sites. Primary data might include:

● interview notes, transcripts, audio or video recordings;
● notes about field observations;

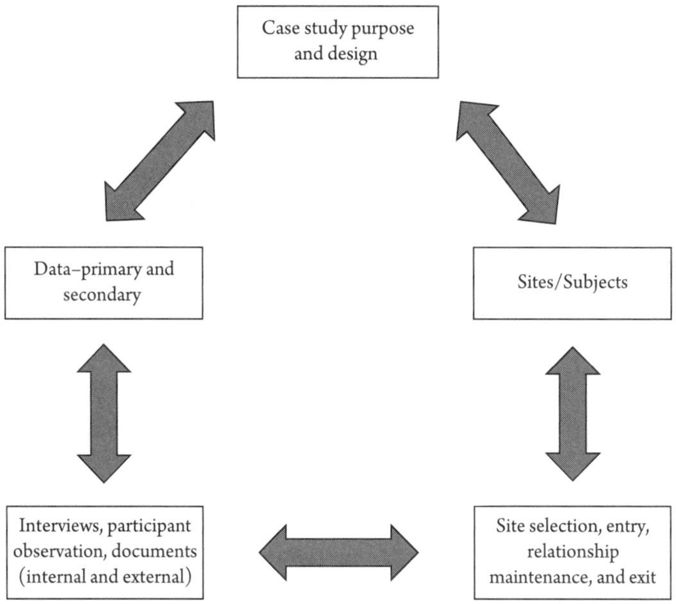

Figure 4.1 Case study purpose and design: reciprocal relationships with issues related to data and site/subject

- reflective data from the subjects in the form of diaries or journals;
- internal or proprietary records (such as organizational memos, financial records, costing data, as well as employee time sheets and other employee records).

Secondary data generally refers to data that is available publically. Depending on the chosen sites, subjects, topics, or issues, there may be sufficient material available in the public domain. Secondary data includes:

- annual reports and other reports submitted to government agencies such as the US Securities Exchange Commission (non-government organizations – NGOs – or non-profit organizations may also be required to submit financial reports or, perhaps, program information to funders for evaluation);
- articles and books;
- transcripts of public meetings including transcripts from court cases;
- multimedia sources including those developed by the organization or those available for Facebook (quasi-public domain) or YouTube videos (public domain);
- databases that might be available in the local or university libraries or through purchase of a relevant database.

Primary data requires attention to developing and maintaining the relationships with the sources.[1] Secondary data requires knowing where to go to get the specific information or garnering the resources to purchase it. Case study methodology generally uses a combination of primary and secondary data. Thus, we need to examine some of the process issues related to the sites in obtaining and utilizing both types of sources. A longer list of primary and secondary data sources appears in Box 4A.1 in the Appendix to this chapter.

4.2 What issues arise in site selection, entry, maintenance, and exit?

Chapter 3 helped us think through our design, including how many units of analysis or sample size we want to target in our study. The general advice is one to less than 30 and more likely an upper limit of 10–12. Eisenhardt (1989) argues that between four and 10 cases work well. We suggest a project including more than 10–12 cases it becomes a very large task to (1) gather data, (2) analyze, (3) develop a coherent understanding, and (4) write up results for publication about the subject *and* its context. An educational course or program or a deadline established by a work setting, grant, or contract may establish time parameters. A researcher must be very cognizant of the time resource available to conduct the research.

Selecting sites or subjects, gaining access, maintaining the relationship, and leave-taking are important and often delicate processes to manage. The larger the number of units we study, the more effort we must devote to these tasks.

Selection

What research sites and individuals within the sites do we want to approach with the request to participate in our research? The identification process can span the gamut from opportunistic or convenience samples to a set of carefully selected subjects. Box 4.1 illustrates the continuum.

BOX 4.1

MODES FOR IDENTIFYING RESPONDENTS OR RESEARCH SITES

$\longleftarrow\longrightarrow$

Opportunistic and convenience samples   Random or purposive/theoretical[a] sampling

Note: a. 'Theoretical sampling' refers to the choice of cases to replicate or extend theory (Eisenhardt, 1989, p. 537).

Opportunistic samples can arise because someone expresses interest in our work and is open to a study. Convenience samples differ somewhat as they include those entities that we can study within the limits of time and resources. We might prefer a site or subject better suited to the purpose of the study, but, that site or subject would take more time to cultivate or more resources than are available. Class projects often fall at this latter end of the continuum.

A case researcher selects sites or subjects on a purposive or theoretical basis. What we mean is that the sites are identified because the site/subject is or contains the phenomenon that we are interested in studying. Purposive or theoretical sampling chooses the subjects or sites that are relevant to the purpose of the study.

One good example of a purposive or theoretical basis for choosing the site is the investigation of the de-institutionalization process at a learning disabilities hospital in Scotland. The process of de-institutionalization had been ongoing in Scotland for over three decades, a rate of change in 'mainstreaming' the clients of institutions that was much slower than in the UK in general. The investigation covered a 20-year period. The time span and the site afforded case researcher Stavros Parlalis (2011) the opportunity to study the process of change in one institution involved in the overall process. Within the organization, however, Parlalis had to decide whom he would interview.

Parlalis used a purposive sample because the issue was a specialized one about which only 'a specific group of professionals. . .would have the appropriate knowledge around the issues investigated' (2011, p. 360). He relied on three key individuals inside the organization to help him identify interviewees with four key characteristics:

- A set of professionals coming from different disciplines (because the diversity of backgrounds and perceptions would enrich the data and help explore it from different perspectives.
- The interviewee's professional status. Thus support staff, nursing assistants, and people with the learning disabilities were not selected.
- The professionals had to be among the individuals who had participated in more than just the last phase of the program.
- The people interviewed had to have worked in the hospital setting and the community so that they would have 'appropriate knowledge and experience for the purposes of this study' (Parlalis, 2011, p. 363).

Case research often has an implied, or explicit, intent to provide insights for practitioners. Researchers may share their insights with participating organizations, a form of action research we will discuss later. Indeed, the best research opportunities are often instances where it is clear to the research sites that they will gain something from the research findings and perhaps from the research process as well. Under what circumstances might individuals or organizations agree to participate in your research program because they foresee value for themselves? There are at least four: consulting, focus group insights, action research, and reflection through ethnographic insights.

Consulting clients

Consulting clients often have potential to become research sites. For example, an entrepreneur who sought psychoanalytic treatment when his marriage was in trouble provided the opportunity for a largely descriptive case study. The insights he garnered from the therapy sessions led to an improved relationship with his wife, other family members, and also with his employees (Kets de Vries, 1996).[2]

Focus group insights

Focus group methodology is an approach that essentially involves group interviewing (e.g., Morgan and Krueger, 1993). Focus groups have been used for multiple purposes including counseling small businesses (e.g., Hutt, 1979); product and program evaluation (e.g., Choe et al., 2006); developing understanding of differing perceptions of hospital staff and patients regarding customer service (e.g., Fottler et al., 2006); ascertaining faculty perceptions regarding e-books for classroom and research uses (e.g., Carlock and Perry, 2008); and identifying employee preferences for benefits, and new product development (e.g., Strang, 2011). Focus group results have been found to provide insights more relevant for managers than other methods of gathering data such as surveys (e.g., Fottler et al., 2006). However, focus groups are most often used by marketing consultants. The transcripts of the dialogue between the moderator and the focus group participants provide the basis for analysis and ultimate recommendations for the client.

One example is the work of Miyauchi and Perry (1999), who undertook a study for the mango industry in Australia, Perry's home country. The purpose was to provide insights for industry participants into why the Japanese consumed very few mangoes and what might be done to increase their consumption of the fruit. Review of the literature indicated insights into Japanese people's preferences for fruit, but nothing regarding mangoes in particular.

The authors conducted four focus groups with Japanese consumers. Two of the groups were individual (in contrast to institutional) fruit buyers and two of the groups consisted of fruit eaters. The questions focused on participants' behaviors and views regarding new and foreign fruits such as mangoes. Three broad research questions guided the interviewing process during the focus group. The questions focused on (1) consumers' views regarding various characteristics of such fruits, (2) aspects that affected increased interest in the fruits, and (3) possible bases on which the market in Japan could be segmented.

With regard to the Japanese consumers' views about the fruit, the authors compared the responses of the Japanese focus group participants with research that had been done with Australian consumers (Miyauchi and Perry, 1999).[3]

Action research

Action research describes research methodology approaches in which the problem and the investigation are intertwined (McFarland and Stansell, 1993). Kurt Lewin (1890–1947), the father of the field of modern social psychology, coined the term 'action research' (Social Psychology Network, 2017). Action research is longitudinal in nature since the methodology compares the unit of analysis before, after the change, and often during the process as well. A typical application of action research involves a number of interactive phases, as Figure 4.2 demonstrates. In action research the researcher may well be a participant in the situation. For example, the researcher may be an employee of the organization that is the research site or head of the organizational unit in which the research is conducted.

Use of action research is extensive. A journal called *Action Research* was founded in 2003. Action research has been frequently used in the field of education as a research approach. In education, an action research project often involves a teacher effecting a change in his or her own classroom. The effort might involve a group of colleagues in multiple classes within a school or even a district-wide effort. In true field experimental mode, a typical project will capture data before the action (or experiment) is undertaken, perhaps at various points in the implementation process, and certainly when the project is completed. The use of an action research approach has spread from education to numerous fields as part of a process for organizational change.

The work of Herguner and Reeves (2000) in a 'Turkish university' (to disguise its real name) illustrates a complex action research design. The

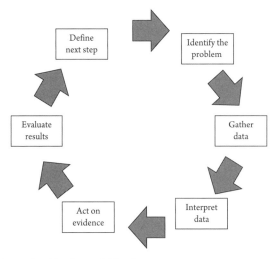

Source: Adapted from Ferrance (2009, p. 9).

Figure 4.2 The interactive phases in the action research process

researchers gathered data measures at three points in time and at two levels in the organization. Although not referred to as action research, the project followed the essence of the prescribed action research process. The university had earlier made the decision to begin offering all of its instruction in English. The two researchers focused on the Language Center, which had a key role in helping to make the transition. The researchers purposed to understand the changes that occurred in various aspects of the university culture when the Language Center implemented total quality management (TQM) in order to improve the Center's service to the university.

Measures of the culture were gathered before implementation began in late 1991 and the same measures were applied in June 1994 at the conclusion of the research period. During the time of the project the researchers gathered multiple sources of data including: interviews, group interviews, observations of the teachers' actions, questionnaires focused on organizational needs administered to the university's teachers, and feedback questionnaires from the students. In addition, a random sample of teachers and students as well as the Center's manager (who was also the lead researcher) kept diaries. The lead researcher subsequently left the university for another position, but returned in early 1998 for a follow-up visit. The visit included administration of one of three questionnaires and observation within the Center. The researchers concluded that 'without leadership and management commitment TQM structures alone may not prevail against national characteristics and prevent a reversion to an earlier organizational culture more typical of the national pattern' (Herguner and Reeves, 2000, p. 55).

Ethnography

Ethnography is formally defined as 'the study and systematic recording of human cultures; *also* a descriptive work produced from such research' (*Merriam-Webster Dictionary*, 2017) or, as Woodside and his colleagues (2012) put it: 'Ethnography is the study of naturally occurring thinking, behavior, and outcomes in real-life contexts [and] includes direct observation and asking open-ended questions face-to-face' (2012, p. 766).

Ethnographic research originated in the field of anthropology with classic works of Bronislaw Malinowski and Margaret Mead. Malinowski (1939 [1944]) studied people in New Guinea early in the twentieth Century.[4] Margaret Mead became, arguably, the most popularly known anthropologists of the twentieth century. Indeed, a whole wing of the American Museum of Natural History in New York City displays parts of her work. Margaret Mead's first book *Coming of Age in Samoa* (1928 [1949]) is still a 'must read' for graduate students interested in applying ethnography to the broader social sciences.[5] Another classic work that used in-depth participant observation work is William Foote Whyte's *Street Corner Society* (1943), which focused on the Italian ethnic area in Boston where Whyte lived.

More recently, ethnographer Jill Kleinberg focused her dissertation research on the kinship ties and economic dynamics of Japanese villages in which the dominant economic activity was pottery making (Kleinberg, 1979; Willhite, 2006). Kleinberg's student, Noriko Yagi, followed her mentor's ethnographic tradition in studying the evolution of the role and changing identification of Japanese citizens who had been sent to take on specific tasks in an American subsidiary of a Japanese firm (Yagi, 2007; Yagi and Kleinberg, 2011).

The ethnographic process is characterized by an intense and often prolonged observation process in situ. The research process also includes in-person interviews and draws on secondary data when such data is available. Mead lived among the Samoan tribes for an extended period, as did Kleinberg in the Japanese mountain village (Willhite, 2006). Whyte lived in the east end of Boston for an extended period developing his in-depth knowledge of the people and their values, interpersonal and intergroup relationships, and their culture. Yagi was a part-time employee of the firm during the time of her fieldwork. The income helped to support her living expenses while she lived in Los Angeles where the Japanese subsidiary was located and also facilitated obtaining insights from the work setting.

During the mid-twentieth century when other fields such as sociology and marketing began to adopt the ethnographic tradition of research, it became 'synonymous with participant observation' (Kelly and Gibbons, 2008, p. 280). We will return to participant observation as a data-gathering process below.

Another way of thinking about the ethnographic methodological process is that the research process aims to develop 'thick description' (Geertz, 1973; Scourfield, 2010, p. 21). Well-known anthropologist Clifford Geertz (1973) utilized the term to transmit the notion that there is more to any given social situation than meets the eye. Thus, to adequately explain any situation requires drawing from the perceptions of multiple participants and from multiple layers in a social system.

Geertz's often cited example is of a Balinese cockfight. By tracing various aspects of the owners of the cocks in the fight, he developed a deeper understanding of the total Balinese community and, in the particular example, of the local politics being played out in the cockfight. One of the humorous stories is how Geertz and his wife were viewing their first Balinese cockfight when the police raided the ongoing illegal activity. The couple dived into a compound with a fellow fugitive they had never met. The compound happened to belong to the fellow spectator whose wife suddenly produced a table, three chairs, tea and refreshments. When the police arrived, the fellow spectator convinced the police that the three certainly had no knowledge about any cockfight and, indeed, had been conversing all afternoon about Geertz's research (Duneier, 2011)! Geertz realized that although he had met very few people during the time he had been there, a network of community participants noted his presence. Further, he came to understand that the cockfights were important for understanding the culture and dynamics of the community.

Geertz's work provides a classic and oft-cited example of case study methodology as his followers note that an aspect of a situation, for example a symbol, is meaningless without accompanying understanding of the larger context. Similarly, a case study researcher focuses on the unit of analysis, but within its context. Ethnographic work and case study methodology share a similar philosophical stance.

In the field of marketing, ethnographic research approaches have been termed consumer immersion, site visits, retail ethnography, shop-alongs, and embedded research (Kelly and Gibbons, 2008, p. 281). In contrast to traditional ethnographic work that might require one or more years in the field, research undertaken in the business fields tend to be much shorter in duration. The intent of such work is to develop an understanding of the meanings and motives behind actions and symbols to individuals. This process has been described as developing an understanding of 'What is it like to be somebody else?' according to Van Maanen (2009, p. 16) and Brannan, Rowe, and Worthington (2012, p. 5). We will return to this interpretivist orientation in Chapter 6. However, a researcher cannot truly develop an understanding without 'thick description'. Thick description comes from in-depth observations and saturation in the unit of analysis and its context. In short, the researcher must experience 'being there'.

Like ethnography, the best case study methodology is based on fieldwork and being physically in situ. At the same time, we want to be quick to note that some case research might rely on secondary data. However, case research that incorporates primary data from the field can yield rich insights. The researcher's insights can be utilized, for example, to inform marketing managers of possible improvements in positioning products and services within their current markets and suggest possible additional markets that might afford potential sales.

Entry, relationship maintenance, and leave-taking of sites and subjects

There are research risks that can occur during the process of seeking access to subjects and sites, as a result of the potential obstacles during the ongoing research, and as one takes exit of a site. These risks cannot be understated, as the example of frustrated doctoral student Randall Rickey indicates. Rickey studied new product development and transition to marketing. On the grant-making board that considered funding for Rickey's proposal was a vice-president of a company. The vice-president complained that the faculty members at Rickey's university were too narrow in their investigations of this process. He insisted that Rickey's proposal be modified to include a firm from his industry. The modified design required study in two firms and the grant was awarded for three years. Firm A, in the industry with which other faculty members had strong relationships, went smoothly for some time. However, late in the research process the firm's contact person became too busy to help arrange the final interviews.

Firm B was the vice-president's own firm. Six months into the research in Firm B, Rickey was told that the ongoing research issues were too strategically sensitive and the firm required that he give the company all research tapes and notes. After some time Rickey was given permission to study the process in Firm C. However, after some months of data gathering, the particular project that Rickey was studying was again (!) deemed too sensitive. Ultimately, after four years of work, Rickey finished his work and his dissertation was approved.[6] Rickey's experience indicates how delicate research relationships can be and that especially interesting topics may be too sensitive for a site to permit access.

Identification of sites and subjects may come from various sources. Our own experiences, as well as those of colleagues, suggest that two major modes of entry occur – the subject seeks you out or you seek the subject. As noted above in the various examples, the site or subject might seek you out because of a need for and expectation of help from your expertise. Such examples are essentially opportunistic in nature. In other instances you may search diligently for the 'right' subject or research site. These latter instances are theoretical matching in nature.

A research program that author Taylor initiated early in her career demonstrates both. She was a member of a foundation board along with Mr. Michael Herman, Senior Vice-President and Chief Financial Officer of Marion Laboratories, a successful Kansas City, Missouri-based pharmaceutical company. Mr. Herman was appreciative of case studies for classroom use and proposed development of a teaching case that focused on his firm. That discussion led to a series of teaching cases initiated with 'Marion Laboratories',[7] which was reprinted widely and became a classic.

The first teaching case focused on the decision of whether to divest Kalo, the company's agricultural subsidiary. At that time in the United States, divestment was not a common strategic choice and, in particular, Kalo's divestment as a management leverage buyout was a new phenomenon. The experience of developing the teaching case piqued author Taylor's interest in the topic of divestment.

Eventually an extensive set of research case studies ensued that was developed primarily through interviews and public documents. The body of work resulted in several papers[8] and ultimately a book. The origin of this work was certainly serendipitous for Taylor, but, the expanding series of case studies that led to the *Divesting Business Units – Making the Decision and Making it Work* (Taylor, 1988) was purposive in nature. Following completion of a series of pedagogical cases on Marion Laboratories, she sought out instances in which companies completed divestitures of subsidiaries. Some of the leads for the case sites came from interviews. Others were identified through publications such as the *Wall Street Journal* or *New York Times*. Author Taylor investigated some of the case studies. Her students developed others. The data underlying this body of work included the interview transcripts; extensive transcripts from the nearly two-day round table involving senior executives who had been involved in divestiture processes; and documents, most of which were from the public domain.

In other instances the relationships begin through work. Yagi is Japanese in origin and is very conscious of relationships among individuals. Her dissertation research focused on one firm. Her article describes how she gained entry:

> The principal investigator [Yagi] knew it is difficult to gain permission from Japanese corporations, even for limited interviews, if one does not have appropriate connections. Narrowing the list of potential sites to corporations with which she had past contact and which currently had expatriate employees at US operations, she chose a corporation where the president of the US subsidiary was a Japanese businessman she had known through her previous job. He agreed to have her visit the company and talk face to face about the project. A month later, she learned that, in addition to allowing her to conduct research, he would provide her with a part-time job so she could communicate with employees in a natural setting. The only stipulation was that he read her dissertation before her defense of it to ensure protection of corporate secrets and image (Yagi and Kleinberg, 2011, p. 637).

Professors from one's past courses as well as thesis or dissertation committee members' relationships with organizations can be immensely helpful in gaining access. However, committee members can also exert influence, which adds risk to the process. Dutch Professor Petra de Weerd-Nederhof put it succinctly when she described the pressure from her supervisor to initiate her research as soon as possible. She moved forward reluctantly. Her reluctance was partly due to the fact that her relative inexperience in working with companies left her with no direct contacts. Nonetheless, she reported with regard to 'the issue of gaining access. I found my in-depth case companies, with no exception, through personal contacts' (2001, p. 526).

In other instances, identification and entry may occur as a result of an indirect connection. Or, the researcher may make a deliberate request for a recommendation from someone who knows both the researcher and someone associated with the site. Other times identification may come from public data and a 'cold call' in the form of a formal request or perhaps 'simply' a telephone call that starts with something like, 'Ms. Stoltenberg, this is

Mikael Søndergaard of Aarhus University. Marilyn Taylor of the University of Missouri at Kansas City suggested I talk with you about a research topic I've been working on for some time'.

Earlier we referred to the process of asking for or being offered a lead on a subject or site as 'snowballing'. Many researchers have effectively used this approach. One example of the snowballing process is the study in the Scottish hospital described above (Parlalis, 2011). Another is the longitudinal case study of the ten-year pre-merger decision process of two hospitals. This study involved 35 interviewees whom Choi and Brommels referred to as 'key informants'. The two authors initiated with the senior managers in the precursor organizations and the hospital that resulted from the merger. The senior managers were asked to identify others who 'had insight into or had been affected by the pre-merger decision-making process' (2009, p. 243).[9]

There are multiple challenges in the process of identifying and entering into research sites. Below we briefly discuss five – managing gatekeepers, determining the level of intimacy needed, remaining astute about confidentiality issues, deciding on overt versus covert entry, and managing the expectations of maintaining a favorable public image.

The first challenge emanates from the fact that gatekeepers control access. Once you have identified a potential site, gaining access is important. In organizations direct access to individuals in senior positions such as Noriko Yagi experienced is not usual. The process of entry requires understanding who the decision-makers are and who the gatekeepers to those individuals are. Author Søndergaard provided this example of his experience with gatekeepers:

> Getting access to do an empirical study in secretive banks and with bankers was a major challenge for me as a PhD student. My first step was to develop an access key or an explanation of the topic that would interest the organization. This move was reflected by the points made by Professor Michel Crozier (1985) on the importance of finding the right balance of interest in order to keep the organization from acting in an abnormal way (European University Institute, May 5th, 1985). The next step was to actually obtain access. I needed gatekeepers. In Denmark, friends from the university in positions in banks were helpful gatekeepers. Bankers who had graduated from the same Master's degree program as I did were also gatekeepers. In France, the needed gatekeepers were world-known professors who provided access either directly to the main bank example in France or to the French Bank Association where the editor of *Revue-Banque* was gatekeeper for additional banks. At my second visit to the French Bank Association the guard at the entrance was

very surprised when I told him I had a meeting with one of the directors of the association. A year earlier I had naively tried to talk with their experts without an appointment and the guard had left me standing on the curb. One bank suggested starting the collaboration with lunch in a golf club in Reims where the branch was located. My example shows that the needed set of gatekeepers may be cultural and industry dependent (Søndergaard, 1990, pp. 124–5).

A researcher can become highly dependent on a gatekeeper. Even with initial success, unforeseen events may still impact on access to the gatekeeper, such as job mobility and death. Further, it is important to retain a degree of control over the when, where, and who you talk to in the course of research.[10]

A second challenge is that the more intimate the insights the researcher wants to develop of the situation, the greater the amount of time the researcher will undoubtedly want to be present in the organization. The greater the level of intimacy needed and the longer the time the researcher feels the need to spend, the greater the challenge of the access process.

Third, confidentiality is often an issue, as the Rickey and Yagi experiences clearly indicate. Professor Rickey ultimately had to gain approval from Company A's legal department – people who were not only busy, but whose job focuses on protecting the company. In Yagi's situation (Yagi and Kleinberg, 2011) the gatekeeper allowed very intimate access, but retained the right to purge the data of confidential information. Similarly De Weerd-Nederhof (2001) found data truncated in some case sites because information about the organizations and their practices was deemed potentially competitively damaging.

The three considerations above emphasize that as a researcher you must tread the delicate balance of being a guest in an organization. In the case of individual subjects, you must remain cognizant that the individual subjects are according you the privilege of entry into a slice of their professional or private lives. Whether your unit of analysis is an organization or an individual, treating that relationship as a privilege is an important aspect of gaining and maintaining trust. Trust is needed in order to obtain the needed information and insights to conduct valid and reliable research. And, even when the researcher has considerable experience and skill, what is going on inside of an organizational site or in an individual subject's life can be disrupted by the research – the danger is very real with all field research and even more so with case research that requires time in situ.

Fourth, overt versus covert entry and data gathering are also important to consider. In an overt process organizational members and potential individual interviewees know of your presence. In a covert entry they do not. Holloway, Brown, and Shipway (2010, p. 80) put it succinctly:

> In a setting where gatekeeper access is not required, the researcher faces the decision as to whether they want participants to be aware of their presence, and to consider the ethical implications of a covert stance. Covert observation is usually considered unethical unless it takes place in public settings and individual participants cannot be identified. There might be occasional exceptions such as situations in which the researcher's identity should not be disclosed in order to safeguard the researcher's safety.

Finally, a frequent delicate balance to manage in the entry process is that the subjects tend to expect a favorable portrait of themselves or of their organizations in the research report and any subsequent publications. One tactic is that the organizational informants simply do not share negative information with the researcher even if the information is germane to the study. Thus, you may not be able to get a balanced picture of an organization. On the other hand those you interview or observe may be quite open, but when the moment comes to ask for permission to release the study for dissemination, the gatekeepers may 'suggest' some significant editing. It is very difficult to stay objective in data gathering and analysis when the organizational gatekeepers want a positive picture with all negative information purged. And, sometimes you just have to walk away.

However, in instances where there may be negative aspects, the importance of anonymity for the informant and the organization cannot be over-emphasized. Professor Rickey pointed out that he felt that he would have had far less difficulty getting the study released if the cases had been disguised. But his committee members insisted that the organizations be identified.

There are exceptions where you might not want to disguise the organization. For example, you might undertake organizational research that focuses on injurious situations with the aim of proposing public policy or private organizational changes. The process of data gathering might rely on public documents and sources outside the organization – or even an internal whistleblower. In the United States at least, there are the risks of being threatened with suits for libel and slander on one hand or pressure to suppress the research on the other hand. For example, author Taylor indicated in a research write-up that the head of the organization was in the hospital for treatment. That information was known outside the company, but not widely.

In what was expected to be the final review stage the company's legal department refused to release the manuscript for publication. Taylor turned to an influential colleague, well known in the company and in political circles in the state. The ultimate compromise was to delete any references to the illness and the work went forward. The delay took several months. The difficulty was similar to Rickey's experience in that the information was considered strategically sensitive and therefore had to be kept from the public domain.

In some instances the researcher, perhaps the supervising committee, or even the institution, are pressured not to publish the research or even complete the research project because of the sensitivity of the focal issue or some information. One compromise solution has been to complete the research, render the thesis or dissertation for committee approval, and then have the institution maintain the document and, perhaps, all of the research materials in a confidential file for an agreed length of time. The drawback for those who have aspirations for an academic career is that the opportunity to publish their findings may be severely truncated. The difficulty is particularly critical if the significance of the insights from the research is time bound.

Overall, then, you must be conscious of the various aspects of the entry process that must be managed. Above all, we have found that patience, persistence, and politeness are important aspects of both managing the entry process and gathering data (see section 4.4). We turn to aspects of the data gathering below.

4.3   What special considerations are important for interviews, participant observation, and documentation?

There are many different sources of data that can be used in a case study project. The Appendix to this chapter is a reasonably comprehensive list, but you may be aware of others. Within the case research domain, the most usual sources of data are interviews, internal and external documents, and observations or participant observations. Some research uses diary approaches in which key individuals keep track of events, and perhaps their reaction to them, over a period of time.

There is a broad, rich literature on data gathering, including books written on interviewing and participant observation in particular. The literature also provides extensive guidance on and examples of content analysis of documents or text that give additional, often implicit, suggestions regarding sources of data. The discussion below simply 'scratches the surface' and invites you to pursue the resources recommended in the references.

Interviews

Interviews can be structured, semi-structured, or unstructured. All use an interview protocol, guide, or schedule even if the questions are very open ended. Larger-scale interview studies that take place within one organization are sometimes titled 'XXXX: A Case Study'. These studies tend to use more structured interview protocols – for example, Nakahara et al. (2009, 2010).[11] Ethnography tends to use unstructured interviews. Case study methodology tends to use 'in-depth interviews' that are semi-structured to unstructured. Even if the interview protocol or guide is unstructured, it may have probe questions – see, for example, Reiter, Stewart, and Bruce (2011).[12] In the main, the unstructured process allows the interviewees to describe the phenomena or to respond to individual questions in their own words and, within the constraints of time, at their own pace. An unstructured interview guided by a skilled interviewer can provide potential for insights into interviewees' feelings, perceptions, emotions, and motivations.

If the interviewee does not permit audio or video recording, you must rely on making notes during the interview. If circumstances prevent writing the notes during the interview, tape-record rough notes from memory as soon as possible after the interview is finished. Author Søndergaard used tape-recorded notes after, in particular, key interviews even if audio-recorded and found it highly useful as it allowed for noting body language and facial expressions as well as other information based on observation.

Even if the interview is audio-recorded, it should be transcribed as soon as possible. This is so that the interviewer can check the transcript and make corrections from memory. An additional step is to make notes of what you remember the interviewee said and then compare the audio-recorded transcript with the handwritten notes. The combination of rough, even fragmentary, audio-recorded notes with the transcript of an audio-recorded interview can often yield a more accurate rendition of the contents of the interview than the transcript alone. Author Søndergaard used both transcripts and notes of interviews he conducted. In particular, he found that the 'small talk' before and after the interview provided fruitful insights and background understanding. Such insights can be included in the analysis.

In the course of our in situ research we have found the following suggestions or considerations helpful:

- In the initial contact with the interviewee, clearly establish the research purpose and your legitimacy. For example, use your university e-mail address rather than your commercial or personal Gmail, Yahoo, or Hotmail personal account. In some cases we have chosen to help a student by sending a formal letter as the faculty supervisor. Such letters indicated the student researcher would call for an appointment.

- If the interviewee will permit a tape recorder, use it. But give the interviewee the tape recorder and tell him or her that he or she can turn it off at any time. A word to the wise here: be sure to keep your notepad handy even if you are using a tape recorder! If the interviewee turns the recorder off, the flow of information provided is likely to be valuable. Even if the interviewee does not want to be quoted, your notes may help in developing themes or constructs. Be judicious about asking to reinitiate a recording process as simply making the request may significantly dampen the insights the interviewee is willing to provide.

- Making at least cursory notes as unobtrusively as possible can be very valuable. Needless to say, fleshing out such notes as soon as possible after the conclusion of the interview is a priority. But, it is better not to sit in your car in the parking lot to make those notes, at least not anywhere near the time you expect the interviewee to leave the building. At least one of us has found ourselves in the embarrassing situation of having the interviewee happen upon us as we were working on notes from an interview that was particularly insightful – but not one that the interviewee necessarily wanted captured verbatim.

- Consider using a video recorder, depending on your longer-term purposes. One reason for using video is that excerpts are often useful for class instruction if you plan to teach a qualitative or case methodology class. Or, you might want to use excerpts for your presentation to your supervising faculty or fellow classmates.

- Decide whether to send an interview schedule in advance. For example, you could send the schedule with the e-mail confirming the appointment or wait to be asked. In either instance, make only a skeletal interview schedule available. In other words, send the version of the interview guide that does not include the probe question.

- Conduct the interview using a two-person team if possible. One person can conduct the interview while the other person takes notes, manages the tape recorder, and makes sure that the planned questions get answered. (Hint: When author Taylor is the one conducting the interview, she usually keeps a notepad handy for use anyway!)[13]

- Do NOT quote anyone and identify that individual by name, title, or any other information that might identify him or her without permission. Different countries may differ with regard to how explicit the permission needs to be. In the United States a written signed document is preferable.

- Use a low-key ice-breaker to open the interview. One that author Taylor finds useful is often the open-ended question 'How did you come to ABC Company?' If the individual is in an advanced position and has been with the company for some time, a good follow-up question is something such as 'You have been with ABC company for xx years [information obtained from the response to the previous question or prior to the interview], how did you come into this position?'

- Try to determine from your gatekeeper or from early interviewees if there are questions or topics that might be particularly sensitive. Unless the logic of the question sequence is severely affected, ask those questions late in the interview. As closing questions, ask:
  - Are there questions I should be asking or issues you feel should be included in the study that were not represented in the questions that have guided our conversation?
  - Are there others I should be interviewing about this topic?[14]

    Send a transcript or even edited notes back to the interviewee with the request to review for additions or corrections. Doing so often leads to a follow-up interview. The follow-up can often be accomplished by phone since the interviewee has vetted you in person during the interview. Make sure you are judicious with regard to the insightful content that the interviewee did not want captured verbatim!

- Send a thank you e-mail or a handwritten note immediately after the interview. Doing so is a good way to continue the trust-building process. In the thank you note make it clear that you will send a transcript for the individual's review. Make sure the individual knows your contact information.

- Send a copy of the manuscript of the study either in draft or finished form depending on promises that have been made. Attaching a handwritten note of thanks can be very meaningful to you and the interviewee. This interaction can also be handled by e-mail, but doing so facilitates premature dissemination. Another option is to send summary results as a courtesy. A third option is to offer an oral presentation regarding the summary observations. But, in all cases, whoever is involved in the case study research is owed the courtesy of receiving a final copy of the case or the publication that includes the case. Note that inviting the feedback during the process provides additional validation[15] that the verbal information provided indeed reflects the interviewee's experiences and opinions. Feedback can provide additional evidence that the researcher has developed a valid and reliable portrayal of the phenomenon. Requesting the feedback also conveys the message that the researcher remains grateful to learn from the interviewee's experiences. Case study research generally cannot provide a basis for statistical support regarding validity and reliability. Rather it relies on your analytical or interpretivist skills in drawing trustworthy observations from the data. However, feedback from the field that says, in essence, 'You got it – you understand the phenomenon from our point of view' is strong evidence that the researcher did indeed 'get it'.

Participant observation

Generally, participant observation is not used in isolation as a means of gathering data and developing understanding of the informants or subjects. An ethnographer noted that '[u]sing the twin methods of participant observation and interviewing offers an unparalleled insight into participants' world' (Holloway et al., 2010, p. 78).[16] Note, however, that there are two words: participant *and* observation. One does not have to be a participant in the organization to make observations. Indeed, observation with minimal participation was a key data source for Gniewosz, about which he said simply, 'Data was collected by observing individuals in their daily activities within their natural environment' (Gniewosz, 1990, p. 224). Gniewosz did, however, ask questions.

Dangers lurk for the participant observer even more than for interviewers. Undertaking participant observation requires time in situ – that is, 'living' in the organization, which characterized the work of ethnographers Mead, Malinowski, Whyte, Kleinberg, and Yagi whose work we described earlier. One danger is 'Stockholm syndrome', a term that has come to mean that an individual adopts the values and viewpoints of long-term captors, referring to a 1973 Stockholm hostage incident. The term came into increased use in the United States after the infamous incident involving heiress Patty Hearst, a kidnap victim who participated in a bank robbery with her abductors during the time she was held captive. Making sure that you regularly talk with someone who remains outside the research site can help maintain your objectivity as the research progresses. Such regular discussions are a useful tactic to help prevent Stockholm syndrome and minimize the resulting bias in interpretation and analysis that can occur (Waclawsky, 2005, p. 62).[17]

A researcher may, of course, be a participant in the organization that is a research site. One example is the manager of the Turkish university Language Center (Herguner and Reeves, 2000) who conducted the action research we described earlier. You will recall that the university had made the strategic decision to deliver its instruction in English and that the Center was charged with facilitating the organizational change. The study followed the implementation of TQM in the Center in order to improve its service to the university community.

Documentation

Documentation can be internal in the form of primary data or external in the form of secondary data. Below we cover each of these separately.

Internal documentation

Internal documents can often be important, even critical, to understanding the phenomenon, its context or even broader system within which the situation has developed or within which the individual functions. Documents such as reports, letters or memos, or personnel records might yield valuable insights. E-mails have provided sources of data for some time, especially if they are 'leaked'. For example, one of our colleagues developed an interesting, and unique, case study of a trail of e-mails between an angry CEO and one of his employees. The e-mail was leaked more broadly in the organization and subsequently became public. The case study provided insights into the organizational culture (Broughton, 2001; Chapman, 2004).[18]

One of the best known business works that relied heavily on internal documents was the classic *Strategy and Structure* (1962) by Pulitzer Prize-winning business historian Alfred Chandler (Chandler, 1962; see also Chandler, 1977; Rodriguez, 2002; Miranti, 2008). This award-winning book included extensive case studies on the evolution of the strategies and accompanying organizational structural arrangements of well-known US firms including DuPont, Standard Oil of New Jersey, Sears Roebuck and General Motors. Dr. Chandler's family was well connected with leading families such as the DuPonts and the Poors. Chandler used set of papers plus other documents that belonged to his deceased great grandfather, the founder of Standard & Poors, as a basis for his history dissertation at MIT. His dissertation was later published in book form (Chandler, 1956). Dr. Chandler is credited with the development of the field of business history. Chandler's body of work relied to a great extent on internal documentation supplemented with secondary data in the form of external publications.

Another rich case study is business historian Mark Fruin's intensive study of Kikkoman, the leading Japan soy sauce manufacturer (Fruin, 1983). Dr.

Fruin's study followed in the tradition of Dr. Chandler under whom he undertook a post-doctorate after finishing his PhD at Stanford. Dr. Fruin relied on historical documents from the company's archives as well as other published materials and some selected interviews. Author Taylor later developed an award-winning case study focused on a later time period and intended for teaching purposes. The case study by Taylor, Tanaka, and Claterbos (2001) drew on Dr. Fruin's work, external contemporary documents such as the company's annual reports as well as practitioner articles, and interviews with senior executives. The teaching case study later became the basis of an analytical article that tracked the development of Kikkoman's distinctive competences (Taylor, Coates, Tanaka, and Claterbos, 2002).

External documents

External documents are materials published in practitioner periodicals and academic journals or available through government based or other public sources. Depending on the purpose of a study and the field for which it is being conducted, a researcher may find that consulting or marketing studies of the company, competitors, or the industry yield valuable data and insights. Electronic databases such as ABI/INFORM, LexisNexis, and Mergent provide powerful search engines to search for data relevant to a particular case study. There is, of course, a wealth of data available via the Web. 'Googling it' has become an important process by which researchers seek, especially preliminary, data and information about a company or even individuals.

The era of increasing utilization of social media has yielded new sources of data. In terms of qualitative research broadly, among the innovative data sources are e-blogs. An example is Valentini and Romenti (2011) who used blogging data to develop insights into the Alitalia crisis that led to that company's privatization. More recently, Facebook and Twitter messages became part of the innovative data sources of the social media. Our prediction is that we will increasingly see case study methodology using social media data sources of information, for example, Wang's (2010) usage of blogs and websites.

One reason is that in the current environment, some appear to have come to equate recency with validity. Students, for example, will seek to utilize data and information found on the web or internet because it is current. In their minds the data and information found here reflects the current situation and thus is a more valid representation of the situation than 'old' data. However, another profound set of issues is important with regard to the sources of data and information. The basic question we need to ask when we draw on data and information from any source is, 'Is it credible?'. Determining the credibility of a data source and the data rendered requires personal judgment. That judgment has to rely on responses to such questions as:

- *Is the author or assembler of the data/information identified?* Anonymous sources have to be viewed with skepticism. Comments about the overall strategy of a firm coming from a lower-level employee have to be weighed carefully. But, on the other hand, observations about the culture and operations of companies by senior executives should be augmented by input from the employees who are living daily within that milieu. Relying on observations from the top of the organization only provides an incomplete and imprecise understanding of the organizational culture (Hofstede, 2001).
- *Is the presentation of the data transparent with regard to where it was gathered from and how it was gathered?* Accounting audit chronicles are replete with stories of questions about reliability of expense reports – an issue we drew to your attention in our discussion of over-reliance on quantitative data. If only summaries of data are available without the original receipts, the validity and reliability of the presentation of the data must be questioned. Typically an auditor will examine at least a sample of the original source documents. In case research, the researcher must at least provide examples of the data. Given limitations on article length, it is difficult to provide readers with full data transparency, but within the limits a researcher must demonstrate raw data, its source, and how it was analyzed and summarized for presentation. Seuring (2008) points, for example, to the lack of documentation of the research process in case study research.
- *Is the conduit that delivered the data/information respected?* Those making entries on internet sites such as blogs often have an axe to grind and thus provide biased data. Publications that are constantly presenting sensational stories with headlines developed to draw the reader's eye must similarly be carefully considered. In the United States, an article from the *Wall Street Journal* will, generally, have more credibility than the weekly so-called 'tabloids' that sit next to checkout stations in retail outlets and have headlines such as 'Kate Flees Murder Scene' (referring to Britain's Duchess of Cambridge) (Reilly, 2012). Such headlines are intended to entice customers standing in line to read and buy. No doubt you can think of publications or sources whose information you place more reliance on than others.

Even information drawn directly from an organization's publicly available documents must be considered judiciously. Information from the company may be valid – it may be a valid portrayal of the company the way the senior executives want their company perceived! Almost invariably, materials issued from an organization emphasize a positive portrayal.

There are multiple reasons that peer-reviewed journals are so strongly weighed in judging the scholarly performance of an academic. The reviewer process is 'blind' and the reviewers generally unknown to the author. The blind review process provides a process that is as free from the bias of cronyism as possible (Notwithstanding authors' relationships with the editor who is known!) Thus, the process affirms the validity and reliability of the information, the methodology by which it was obtained and analyzed, the synergism between the results and the author's conclusions, and the lack of obvious bias in the author's rendition of the data, analysis, and conclusions. The process affirms reliability and validity. However, simultaneously, the process of review and revision often leads to a significant delay in the delivery of data/information to public review – diminishing the usability or relevance of the data/information.

As authors we are empathetic with graduate student's dilemmas of whether to draw on valid information as judged by recency or on information/data from sources that have been carefully vetted for reliability and validity but may not be very current. Which to use depends upon the purpose of the research project at hand. A program leading to a Master's level thesis by a student aiming for a PhD program should certainly utilize articles from peer-reviewed journals but, depending on the purpose and design of the study, is likely to also draw on data that is current. A case study for a course in which the assignment is to analyze an organization's current situation requires more reliance on the criterion of recency and little reliance on peer-reviewed publications that often contain information several years old.

The important point is to be as aware as possible of the reliability and validity of the source – the recency factor should be self-evident. Reliability and validity are more difficult to ascertain regarding recent sources and often have to rely on the reputation of the source.

4.4   Patience, persistence, and politeness

For case study research, the lessons to be learned from Dr. Xiaohua Yang's example below are patience, persistence, and politeness. All three are key aspects of developing relationships that permit in-depth information that is both valid and reliable. The research initiated with a case study project in order to understand the phenomenon in situ. The major portion of the data gathering, however, was not a case study project, but the administration of an extensive questionnaire.

In the course of the research, Xiaohua Yang focused on managing the data-gathering process. Her supervisors concurred that her process for managing her research process was one of the best they had ever experienced. First, she sent an advance letter to the targeted respondent on university letterhead. The letter clearly identified that copies were sent to her supervisors, each of whom had senior faculty roles in their university. Second, she sent a priority package containing a brief second letter and the questionnaire along with a large return-address stamped envelope. Third, if she did not get a response after a two-week interval, she called personally and fourth sent a follow-up package. In the phone call she indicated that she anticipated that the first package somehow did not reach the recipient. The questionnaire was lengthy and response rates on such questionnaires are often quite low. Her response rate was high and at 55 percent was rare indeed. A decade later, Dr. Yang might have offered the respondents opportunity to complete the information online or in written form (Yang, Taylor, and Stoltenberg, 1999).

4.5   A final word

This chapter has provided basic guidance regarding the research sites, data and information sources you will use in your research. If your design calls for the use of primary data, you will need to carefully consider the sites and/or subjects that will be the sources of your information. Entry into organizations and development of relationships with individuals in case research are critical processes that must be carefully managed. Even when the researcher has considerable experience and skill, there are risks of delay to the research process – or cessation of the research entirely. During the course of the research and even in the post-publication period maintenance of the integrity of the relationships with your sources of primary data is important. Finally, the sources of secondary data also require judicious attention. The integrity of the data is critical in order to assure validity and reliability of results. True, recency is often important even critical, but trying to understand an organization's *current* situation may require astute consideration of the biases in data you assemble to utilize for your analysis.

? END OF CHAPTER QUESTIONS AND ANSWERS

1 **What are the differences between primary and secondary data?** Primary and secondary data differ in approaches to data and the degree of control of data collection. Primary data is direct or first-hand evidence supplied directly from the site or from the subject to the

researcher. It is the researcher who conducts primary data collection. The primary data is gathered for the purpose for which it was intended. Secondary data is second-hand evidence available from the public domain or private source. The data is not collected by the researcher and is collected for a different purpose. The researcher controls the primary data collection while the collection of secondary data is outside the domain of control available to the researcher.

2 **What issues arise in site selection, entry, maintenance and exit?** Selection or identifying the sites or subject of study may derive from difference sources. The subject may seek you out with an expectation of assistance (e.g., consulting clients) or you may seek out the subject and site for research purposes (e.g., purposive or theoretical sampling). An opportunistic or convenience selection may take place. Once the selection is made, one challenge to address is finding and handling gatekeepers who control the access. Recommended entry, and snowballing selection, may be an effective way of getting access to sources. Besides maintaining gatekeepers, and deciding on overt versus covert entry and data gathering, a challenge is determining the level of intimacy needed. The more intimate the insights the researcher seeks, the greater amount of time will the case researcher need to be present in the organizational context. Other challenges are remaining astute about confidentiality issues and managing the expectations of maintaining a favorable public image. It is important to be conscious about the various possible steps in the entry process that must be managed. We found that patience, persistence, and politeness are important elements in both managing the entry process and gathering the data.

3 **What special considerations are important for interviews, participant observation, and documentation?** Regarding interviews, a protocol or guide is used regardless of the degree of structure the interview has. Participant observation provides, in addition to interviewing, insights by observing individuals or phenomena in their daily activities within their natural context with minimal participation. Dangers lurk for the participant observer even more than for interviewers. Regarding the types of documentation, internal forms of documentation can be primary data. External forms of documentation can be secondary data. Electronic databases provide powerful search engines to search for data relevant to a particular case study. 'Googling it' has become an important process by which researchers seek, especially preliminary data and information about a company or even individuals. Social media have yielded new sources of data and innovative data sources such as e-blogs, Facebook and Twitter. For all types of data it is important to ask whether the source is credible. It is a matter of personal judgment to determine the credibility of a data source. Such judgment can be facilitated by answering questions such as:

(a) Is the author or assembler of the data/information identified? The reason for asking this question is because anonymous sources have to be viewed with skepticism.

(b) Is the presentation of the data transparent with regard to where it was gathered from and how it was gathered?

(c) Is the conduit that delivered the data/information respected? Entries on internet sites such as blogs often have an axe to grind and therefore provide biased data. Even information drawn directly from an organization's publicly available documents must be considered judiciously.

NOTES

1 Two unusual sources of primary data are (a) a reflective narrative that provided the data for the economic study of a consumer's auto-buying experiences based on a written report from participant observation (Earl, 2012); and (b) the experience of Professor Kets de Vries who utilized his extensive notes as a therapist for an entrepreneur to develop an entrepreneurial profile (Kets de Vries, 1996).

2 In Kets de Vries (1996) the client came with concerns about his marriage. The therapy sessions revealed that some of his behaviors 'affected the way he ran the business. . . [and] influenced his relationships

with customers and suppliers. And at times. . .led to disastrous action' (p. 863). Through the therapy, as is characteristic of psychoanalytic treatment, the entrepreneur began to recognize that interactions with and reactions to his nuclear family members during his early life contained the roots of some of the dysfunctional behaviors that were affecting his relationship with his wife and other family members. These dynamics were also affecting his business and relationships with employees. The client was willing to undertake behavioral changes in the light of the insights he developed as a result of the therapy sessions. Better relationships with his wife and mother as well as employees and other business associates resulted. However, Professor Kets de Vries never reported whether the company became more profitable. The one evidence of impact on the organization as a whole was that the client initiated succession planning that led to conversations with his son and a development plan for the son to eventually become head of the firm.

3 In Chapter 5, which focuses on analysis, we will refer to this analysis process as 'pattern matching'. Note that Miyauchi and Perry say that 'the Japanese consumers view mangoes as foreign and new fruit. Therefore, characteristics such as taste and physical aspects (for example, a large seed and smell) and the way to eat mangoes are unfamiliar to Japanese consumers' (1999, n.p.). With regard to consumers' views of fruit characteristics, general literature indicated what 'Japanese consumers favour in fruit in general: taste, freshness, way of eating, uniqueness, presentation, and product quality' (*ibid.*). Miyauchi and Perry were able to compare these previous findings with the perceptions of the focus group participants. Segmentation insights included possibilities to appeal to young people, positioning of mangoes as gift items, and typical attitudes toward trying new fruits. For managers involved in the mango industry the insights were expected to help increase sales in Japan. In particular, the authors suggested that the managers of marketing functions in the industry should target: 'young people (i.e., an age segment); housewives (buying role); those who have never tasted mangoes (user status); those who seek nutrition from fruit (benefit sought); those with positive attitude towards foreign fruit (attitude); and gift use, food industry use, and household use (occasion)' (*ibid.*). Note: the research was not longitudinal, thus, we do not know if (a) the mango industry participants who received the study undertook the recommended changes in positioning of the fruit in Japan; and (b) if so, whether increased sales resulted.

4 Malinowski's most famous works were anthropological description and interpretations. See Malinowski (1922 [1966]; 1935 [1966]; 1949).

5 See also Mead (1972).

6 At the request of 'Professor Rickey' this experience has been disguised. References included (a) discussions with Professor Rickey; (b) a synopsis of the experience; (c) the dissertation abstract; and (d) the dissertation.

7 See Taylor (1982), Taylor and Kinker (1982), and Taylor, Kinker, and Garland (1982).

8 See Taylor, Narayanan, and Kinker (1983, 1984); Taylor (1985, 1988); and Taylor, Taylor, and Hooper (1987, 1988).

9 Author Taylor regularly has her students use the following question as part of an interview schedule: 'Who else should we be talking with about this issue?' Including this question potentially provides two important pieces of information: (a) evidence that the set of interviewees is appropriate and (b) suggested additions. It is a form of 'snowballing', a sampling process for which the aim is to choose the initial unit on the basis of a theoretical match, that is, a match to the focal issue. Sandström and Carlsson (2008) describe how they used the snowballing technique in a study of networks: 'The basic idea of the snowballing interview technique is to identify the networks inductively, letting the respondents nominate each other as being parts of the network (Miles and Huberman, 1994). Within each network, the interviews started with two presumably central actors (i.e., those persons assigned as coordinators) and continued until no new actor was identified as having any central role in the performance of any of the organizing functions. Based on the information given, the snowballing ends when the above criterion is met. In total, 24 respondents were interviewed. The interview sessions lasted from 30 to 90 minutes. A tape recorder was used, and each interview was transcribed for the purpose of qualitative analysis. The interviews provided data regarding the set of actors involved, how the organizing processes were carried out, and general information about the performance of the networks – meaning their level of efficiency and innovativeness. The judgments concerning these issues as related to determining performance were made based on the aggregated information reported by the respondents' (Sandström and Carlsson, 2008, n.p.).

10 Award-winning author and researcher Dr. Harry Levinson, then of Harvard Business School, supervised author Taylor and a set of fellow graduate students through an organizational analysis case study. Dr.

Levinson made this analogy: 'A researcher is akin to a medical doctor making rounds in the hospital. The doctor does not want to be led by the elbow by a nurse, no matter how competent the nurse may be.' The independence of the researcher (or doctor) is critical, as Professor Levinson's comment suggests. But, the researcher cannot demand independence. One might make the analogy of being a guest in a home. The host might initially make you welcome in the living room and formal dining room. Entry to the family room and kitchen may have to wait until later – and exploration of the bedrooms may remain permanently off limits!

11 For an interesting example see Nakahara et al. (2010, n.p.). These authors used a 'stratified two-stage cluster systematic random sampling with probability proportional to size. The team first stratified Cambodian provinces by population density into three strata. They then undertook a sampling in each stratum with the probability dependent on the health care centers present in the strata. The researchers interviewed representatives from 84 health centers and 17 referral hospitals by telephone using a structured interview schedule or sent them a questionnaire'. Their methodology is explained more thoroughly in Nakahara et al. (2009).

12 For arguments regarding systematic, yet flexible research approaches see Reiter et al. (2011), who argue: 'Research addressing current management issues requires both a flexible framework and the capability to consider the research problem from various angles [in] qualitative research. . .it is not always immediately clear which is the most appropriate method to use, as the research objectives shift and crystallize over time' (p. 35).

13 Taylor has the unique skill of being able to take notes in shorthand while keeping eye contact most of the time. The notes are rough and need to be edited, corrected, and elaborated immediately after the interview. It has proved to be a useful skill.

14 The first of the two questions helps the researcher to ascertain whether the topical boundaries of the investigation should be enlarged or provides suggestions for future research. The second question helps to (a) affirm that the set of individuals being interviewed are appropriate and (b) provides recommendations regarding individuals who might provide additional perspectives about the phenomenon under study if there is time. The second question is essentially a variation of the snowball technique described earlier in this chapter.

15 There are scholars who determinedly argue that seeking validation from study participants, such as interviewees, is totally inappropriate.

16 Holloway et al. refer to Spindler (1982), Gilbert (1993), Denzin (1997), Denzin and Lincoln (1998), Seale (1999), Hammersley and Atkinson (2007), and Fetterman (2010).

17 Waclawsky (2005, p. 62) notes that: 'The "Stockholm Syndrome" describes the behavior of some hostages. The "System Standards Stockholm Syndrome" describes the behavior of system standards participants who, over time, become addicted to technology complexity and hostages of group thinking. . . Although the original name derives from a 1973 hostage incident in Stockholm, Sweden, the expanded name and its acronym, S^4, applies specifically to systems standards participants who suffer repeated exposure to cult dogma contained in working group documents and plenary presentations. By the end of a week in captivity, Stockholm Syndrome victims may resist rescue attempts, and afterwards refuse to testify against their captors. In system standards settings, S^4 victims have been known to resist innovation and even refuse to compete against their competitors'.

18 In addition, author Taylor was privy to a private communication with the case study author, Dr. John Bunch then of Benedictine College. Bunch developed the case study on the original e-mail and the series of e-mails that followed. The CEO Neal Patterson had sent the original e-mail to an employee. The original e-mails had a very angry tone. According to Patterson, a Harvard professor delayed publication of a book that contained the e-mail. There was no explanation as to why. Perhaps the company put pressure on Harvard. But the implication was that companies interested in favorable images can and may indeed subject a researcher to pressure to withdraw or change data or information that has been obtained during the course of a case study research. Certainly the instance of Professor Rickey's doctoral dissertation research process indicates the influence of organizational participants on the course of research!

REFERENCES

Brannan, M., M. Rowe, and F. Worthington (2012), 'Time for a new journal, a journal for new times', *Journal of Organizational Ethnography*, **1**(1), 5–14.

Broughton, P.D. (2001, April 6), 'Boss's angry email sends shares plunging', *The Telegraph*.

Carlock, D.M and A.M. Perry (2008), 'Exploring faculty experiences with e-books: A focus group', *Library Hi Tech*, **26**(2), 244–54.

Chandler, A. (1956), *Henry Varnum Poor: Business Editor Analyst and Reformer*, Cambridge, MA: Harvard University Press.

Chandler, A.D. (1962), *Strategy and Structure*, Cambridge, MA: MIT Press.

Chandler, A.D. (1977), *The Visible Hand*, Cambridge, MA: The Belknap Press of Harvard University Press.

Chapman, C. (2004), 'Cerner CEO predicts workplace changes', *Achieve*, William Jewell College.

Choe, P., C. Kim, M.R. Lehto, X. Lehto, and J. Allebach (2006), 'Evaluating and improving a self-help technical support web site: Use of focus group interviews', *International Journal of Human–Computer Interaction*, **21**(3), 333–54.

Choi, S. and M. Brommels (2009), 'Logics of pre-merger decision-making processes: The case of Karolinksa University Hospital', *Journal of Health Organization Management*, **23**(2), 240–54.

Crozier, M. (1985), Seminar, European University Institute, Florence, 5 May.

Denzin, N. (1997), *Interpretive Ethnography: Ethnographic Practices for the 21st Century*, Thousand Oaks, CA: Sage.

Denzin, N. and Y. Lincoln (1998), *Collecting and Interpreting Qualitative Materials*, Thousand Oaks, CA: Sage.

De Weerd-Nederhof, P.C. (2001), 'Qualitative case study research. The case of a PhD research project on organizing and managing new product development systems', *Management Decision*, **39**(7), 513–38.

Doyle, A.C. (1892), *The Adventure of the Copper Beeches*, first published in *Strand Magazine* .

Duneier, M. (2011), 'How not to lie with ethnography', *Sociological Methodology*, **41**(1), 1–11.

Earl, P.E. (2012), 'Experiential analysis of automotive consumption', *Journal of Business Research*, **65**(7), 1067–72.

Eisenhardt, K.M. (1989), 'Building theories from case study research', *The Academy of Management Review*, **14**(4), 532–50.

'Ethnography' (2017), *Merriam-Webster Dictionary* accessed 3 February 2017 at https://www.merriam-webster.com/dictionary/ethnography.

Ferrance, E. (2000), *Themes in Education: Action Research*, LAB, a program of the Education Alliance, Northeast and Islands Regional Educational Laboratory, Brown University, Providence, Rhode Island, accessed 3 February 2017 at http://www.brown.edu/academics/education-alliance/sites/brown.edu.academics.education-alliance/files/publications/act_research.pdf.

Ferrance, E. (2009), *Action Research*, LAB/Northeast and Islands Regional Educational Laboratory. Brown University, accessed 21 June 2017 at https://www.brown.edu/academics/education-alliance/sites/brown.edu.academics.education-alliance/files/publications/act_research.pdf.

Fetterman, D.F. (2010), *Ethnography: Step by Step*, 3rd edition, Thousand Oaks, CA: Sage.

Fottler, M.D., D. Dickson, R.C. Ford, K. Bradley, and L. Johnson (2006), 'Comparing hospital staff and patient perceptions of customer service: A pilot study utilizing survey and focus group data', *Health Services Management Research*, **19**(1), 52–66.

Fruin, W.M. (1983), *Kikkoman: Company, Class, and Community*, Cambridge, UK: Harvard University Press.

Geertz, C. (1973), 'Thick description: Toward an interpretive theory of culture', *The Interpretation of Cultures*, New York: Basic Books, pp. 3–30.

Gilbert, N. (1993), *Researching Social Life*, Thousand Oaks, CA: Sage.

Gniewosz, G. (1990), 'The share investment decision process and information use: An exploratory case study', *Accounting and Business Research*, **20**(79), 223–30.

Hammersley, M. and P. Atkinson (2007), *Ethnography Principles in Practice*, London: Taylor & Francis.

Herguner, G. and N.B.R. Reeves (2000), 'Going against the national cultural grain: A longitudinal case study of organizational cultural change in a Turkish higher education', *Total Quality Management*, **11**(1), 45–66.

Hofstede, G. (2001), *Culture's Consequences*, 2nd edition, Thousand Oaks, CA: Sage.

Holloway, I., L. Brown, and R. Shipway (2010), 'Meaning not measurement: Using ethnography to bring a deeper understanding to the participant experience of festivals and events', *International Journal of Event and Festival Management*, **1**(1), 74–85.

Hutt, R.W. (1979), 'The focus group interview: A technique for counseling small business clients', *Journal of Small Business Management*, **17**(1), 15–18.

Kelly, D. and M. Gibbons (2008), 'Marketing methodologies ethnography: The good, the bad and the ugly', *Journal of Medical Marketing*, **8**(4), 279–85.

Kets de Vries, M.F.R. (1996), 'The anatomy of the entrepreneur: Clinical observations', *Human Relations*, **49**(7), 853–83.

Kleinberg, M.J. (1979), 'Kinship and economic growth: Pottery production in a Japanese village', dissertation, University of Michigan.

'Kurt Lewin' (2017), Social Psychology Network, accessed 12 March 2017 at https://www.social psychology.org/social-figures.htm.

Malinowski, B. (1939 [1944]), *A Scientific Theory of Culture and Other Essays*, Chapel Hill, NC: University of North Carolina Press.

Malinowski, B. (1949), *Crime and Custom in Savage Society*, London: Routledge.

Malinowski, B. (1922 [1966]), *Argonauts of the Western Pacific. An Account of Native Enterprise and Adventure in the Archipelagoes of Melanesian New Guinea*, London: Routledge and Kegan Paul.

Malinowski, B. (1935 [1966]), *Coral Gardens and their Magic, Vol. I: Soil-Tilling and Agricultural Rites in the Trobriand Islands*. London: Allen and Unwin.

McFarland, K.P. and J.C. Stansell (1993), 'The teacher as researcher: Historical perspectives', in L.S. Patterson (ed.), *Teachers are Researchers: Reflection in Action*, Newark, DE: International Reading Association, pp. 12–18.

Mead, M. (1928 [1949]), *Coming of Age in Samoa*, New York: Mentor.

Mead, M. (1972), *Blackberry Winter: My Earlier Years*. New York: Simon & Schuster.

Miles, M.B. and M.A. Huberman (1994), *Qualitative Data Analysis – An Expanded Sourcebook*, 2nd edition, Thousand Oaks, CA Sage Publications.

Miranti, P.J. (2008), 'Chandler's paths of learning', *Business History Review*, **82**(2), 293–300.

Miyauchi, Y. and C. Perry (1999), 'Marketing fresh fruit to Japanese consumers: Exploring issues for Australian exporters', *European Journal of Marketing*, **33**(1/2), 196–205.

Morgan, D.L. and R.A. Krueger (1993), 'When to use focus groups and why', in D.L. Morgan (ed.), *Successful Focus Groups: Advancing the State of the Art*, Thousand Oaks, CA: Sage.

Nakahara, S., S. Saint, S. Sann, M. Ichikawa, and A. Kimura et al. (2010), 'Referral systems for injured patients in low-income countries: A case study from Cambodia', *Health Policy and Planning*, **25**(4), 319–27.

Nakahara, S., S. Saint and S. Sann, R. Phy, and M. Ichikawa et al. (2009), 'Evaluation of trauma care resources in health centres and referral hospitals in Cambodia', *World Journal of Surgery*, **33**(5), 874–85.

Parlalis, S.K. (2011), 'Management of organisational changes in a case of de-institutionalization', *Journal of Health Organization and Management*, **25**(4), 355–84.

Reilly, J. (2012), 'Is this the most tasteless cover in history? US magazine Globe claims Queen "is dying and Camilla has evil plot to claim throne"', accessed 3 March 2017 at http://www.dailymail.co.uk/news/article-2228064/US-magazine-Globe-claims-Queen-dying-Camilla-evil-plot-claim-throne.html.

Reiter, S., G. Stewart, and C. Bruce (2011), 'A strategy for delayed research method selection: Deciding between grounded theory and phenomenology', *Electronic Journal of Business Research Methods*, **9**(1), 35–46.

Rodriguez, J.N. (2002), 'Strategy and structure redux', *Business Strategy Review*, **13**(3), 20–27.

Sandström, A. and L. Carlsson (2008), 'The performance of policy networks: The relation between network structure and network performance', *Policy Studies Journal*, **36**(4), 497–524.

Scourfield, P. (2010), 'I haven't forgotten about you', *Qualitative Research Journal*, **10**(2), 20–35.

Seale, C. (1999), *The Quality of Qualitative Research*, Thousand Oaks, CA: Sage.

Seuring, S.A. (2008), 'Assessing the rigor of case study research in supply chain management', *Supply Chain Management*, **13**(2), 128–37.

Søndergaard, M. (1990), 'På Sporet af den nationale kulturs konsekvenser, En sammenligning af praksis i danske og franske pengeinstitutetter, den nationale kulturs betydning' [In search of national cultures' consequences. A comparison of practices in Danish and French banks, the significance of national culture], unpublished PhD thesis, Aarhus Business School.

Spindler, G. (1982), *Doing the Ethnography of Schooling*, New York: CBS.

Strang, K.D. (2011), 'A grounded theory study of cellular phone new product development', *International Journal of Internet and Enterprise Management*, **7**(4), 366–87.

Taylor, M.L. (1982), 'Marion Laboratories, Inc.', *Case Research Journal*, **II**, 105–30.

Taylor, M.L. (1985), 'Managing divestiture effectively', in L. Fahey (ed.), *Strategic Planning Management*, Chicago, IL: Communique, Inc., pp. 1–6.

Taylor, M.L. (1988), *Divesting Business Units – Making the Decision and Making it Work*, Lexington, MA: Lexington Books.

Taylor, M. and D. Kinker (1982), 'Kalo, Inc.', *Proceedings*, Case Research Association, November.

Taylor, M., T.T. Coates, N. Tanaka, and J. Claterbos (2002), 'Foreign market entry – the U.S. and beyond: Kikkoman's globalization through the RBV and C2 perspectives', *Current Issues in Management*, **2**, 78–97.

Taylor, M., D. Kinker, and J. Garland (1982), 'American Stairglide, Inc.', *Proceedings*, Case Research Association.

Taylor, M.L., V.K. Narayanan, and D. Kinker (1983), 'Strategic management of divestment in the United States', Society for Strategic Management, Paris.

Taylor, M., N. Tanaka and J. Claterbos (2001), 'Kikkoman', *Case Research Journal*, **21**(3), 1–28.

Taylor, M., N. Taylor and F. Hooper (1987), 'Why diversified firms voluntarily divest ongoing business units: Modeling the corporate divestment decision', *Proceedings*, Southern Management Association, pp. 208–10.

Taylor, M., N. Taylor and F. Hooper (1988), 'Predicting divestment from corporate level data', *Proceedings*, Decision Sciences Institute-Northeast.

Taylor, M., V.K. Narayanan, and D. Kinker (1984), 'Factors involved in divestment effectiveness', *Proceedings*, Southern Management Association, pp.116–18.

Valentini, C. and S. Romenti (2011), 'Blogging about crises', *Journal of Communication Management*, **15**(4), 298–313.

Van Maanen, J. (2009), 'Ethnography then and now', *Qualitative Research in Organizations and Management: An International Journal*, **1**(1), 13–21.

Waclawsky, J.G. (2005), 'S⁴ – The System Standards Stockholm Syndrome', *Business Communications* Review, **35**(7), 62.

Wang, T.-L. (2010), 'A comparative study of campaign blogs and web sites: The case of Taiwan's 2008 general election', *Online Information Review*, **34**(2), 229–49.

Whyte, W.F. (1943), *Street Corner Society: The Social Structure of an Italian Slum*, Chicago, IL: University of Chicago Press.

Willhite, J. (2006), 'An interview with Jill Kleinberg', November 28, Oral History Project, Endacott Society, University of Kansas, accessed 12 March 2017 at http://www.kuonlinedirectory.org/ endacott/data/OralHistoryTranscripts/Jill%20Kleinberg.pdf.

Woodside, A.G, E. Ko, and H. Tzung-Cheng (T.C.) (2012), 'The new logic in building isomorphic theory of management decision realities', *Management Decision*, **50**(5), 765–77.

Yagi, N. (2007), 'When are the Japanese "Japanese"?': Negotiating cultural identities in a Japan–United States binational organization', dissertation, University of Kansas.

Yagi, N. and J. Kleinberg (2011), 'Boundary work: An interpretive ethnographic perspective on negotiating and leveraging cross-cultural identity', *Journal of International Business Studies*, **42**(5), 629–53.

Yang, X., M. Taylor, and C. Stoltenberg (1999), 'Assessing the effects of structural and project characteristics on R&D strategic alliance', *Journal of High Technology Management Research*, **10**(1), 105–21.

Yin, R.K. (2009), *Case Study Research: Design and Methods*, 4th edition, Thousand Oaks, CA: Sage.

Appendix

BOX 4A.1

DATA SOURCES FOR CASE STUDY RESEARCH

Primary data sources

Interviews, including: in-depth, focused, structured and unstructured
Portfolios
Samples of work output
Diaries or journals
Field notes
Observations including: use of formal study protocols, formal or informal meetings within the organizational setting
Informal conversations
Researchers' reflections
Participation observation: passive (e.g., as a neighbor or a member of the organization), insider view
Audiotapes
Videotapes
Photos
Focus groups
Anecdotal records
Internal documents: memos, individual files, logs of meetings, internal records including test results, report cards (educational organizations) and consulting reports
Financial records: data, reports, financial accounting, managerial accounting
Project reports
Self-assessments
Case studies
Checklists: attendance records, agreement/disagreement (e.g., with a decision or opinion)
Questionnaires: a priori/published or developed for the organizational purpose
Surveys: telephone, mail/e-mail/Internet based, in person
Performances: live or recorded

Secondary or publicly available information

Industry data
Published articles regarding:
   The industry
   The organization
   Individuals in the organization
   Technology changes
Annual reports, 990s (financial reports from non-profit organizations), or other periodic reports to external stakeholders

Source: List of examples adapted from Ferrance (2000, p. 11) with augmentation from Yin (2009, p. 102).

5

Dealing with the dilemmas of case analysis

> It is a capital mistake to theorize before one has data. Insensibly one begins to twist facts to suit theories, instead of theories to suit facts.
> (Sherlock Holmes, *A Scandal in Bohemia*)

> Having gathered these facts, Watson, I smoked several pipes over them, trying to separate those which were crucial from others which were merely incidental.
> (Sherlock Holmes, *The Crooked Man*)

LEARNING OBJECTIVES

To help understand and move forward in the analysis process in case study research, this chapter responds to the following questions:

1 Why is there often a delay between data gathering and completion of data analysis?

2 How do content analysis and QDAs help case study research?

3 What various forms of data coding can be used in case study research?

4 How does Robert Yin suggest we go about analyzing our case study data?

Once the case research data is complete or nearly completed, the next step is analysis. Author Søndergaard in the account below notes that data does not speak for itself. Analysis and interpretation are critical to drawing out 'the truth' – or, in case research 'the reality' (Watts, 2007). In undertaking a case-based research process, the analysis should be ongoing throughout. However, after the data gathering is completed, the researcher's emphasis will be on analysis, the focus of this chapter. Comparatively speaking, the instructions for the previous stages of developing the case study described in the earlier chapters are fairly well developed. The instructions and guidance for the analysis of case-based research data are, however, still relatively under-developed. Indeed, this process is considered to be the most difficult aspect of doing case study research.

Why is analyzing data from case study research a difficult task? In this chapter we provide several examples and advice from case researchers who have 'been there' in terms of the challenges and successes.

5.1 Why is there often a delay between data gathering and completion of data analysis?

Below, author Søndergaard recounts some of the difficulties he encountered in getting sites and data for his dissertation and how he was finally able to break through the analysis roadblock:

> My doctoral dissertation was case-based and my research question was: How do national cultural differences reflect in behavior differences in business organiza-tions? The research question required a carefully designed selection of case evi-dence in order to control for other factors that could influence behaviors.
>
> I used functional equivalence and matched pairs as the primary basis for select-ing the organizations to participate. I needed similar organizations – commercial banks – similar organizational units – in similar customer contexts – with similarly highly esteemed bankers. In the structured interviews I asked each interviewee questions regarding a hypothetical loan decision. The questions were designed to understand the different roles in the organizational hierarchy. The unit of analysis was the critical event in which the decision required that the formal delegated authority needed to be exceeded for good reasons.
>
> Developing the design of the case research project took a lot of time because I had to gain an understanding of the real life context of commercial banks and loan decision-making. Getting access to the banks took even longer and required a lot of help of people in high places and from trusting friends. After a lot of hard work to obtain access, I was able to complete over 100 recorded interviews in eight commercial banks in Denmark and France. The transcripts formed the case evidence.
>
> I believed that the data 'talked' by itself, that the results were self-evident. However, it was a long time before the data started 'talking' and others could concur with my interpretations.
>
> What happened? Well, the breakthrough occurred in August 1989 when Robert Yin spoke at a case research workshop on the Sandbjerg Estate (the conference center of Aarhus University) located in the southern part of Jutland, Denmark. This visit occurred in August 1989 and was the first time ever Yin travelled outside of the United States. The data started talking as I applied a technique of analyzing

case evidence that Yin talked about. The analysis enabled data to speak to others as well as myself, most importantly my dissertation committee! (Søndergaard, 1990, pp. 5–16)

Because of the many challenges in developing the research questions, designing the data collection process, and gaining access to the needed data, the choice of process for analyzing the data is often neglected until the researcher senses its imminence. Author Søndergaard's account illustrates the difficulties. In case-based research, significant time may pass before the data begins to make sense, as in author Søndergaard's example.

In spite of the significant guidance provided by Yin and others over an extended period of time, there is still no 'cookbook' approach to analysis of case evidence. Yin has stressed this lack of guidance for multiple decades,[1] even as he has continued to develop guidance for the case research analysis process. Professor Petra de Weerd-Nederhof talked about how she went about the analysis process of her case study-based dissertation in Box 5.1.

Whatever approach you select to analyze the data, that process must enable the case evidence to talk to a broader audience, broader than you the researcher. The approach chosen must include transparency of the analysis process and must yield conclusions that are accepted as valid and trusted by your academic and practitioner supervisors.

The novice case study researcher will search for definitive formulas, recipes, tools, and other techniques that will produce the needed analytical results.

BOX 5.1

PROFESSOR DE WEERD-NEDERHOF ON THE IMPORTANCE OF THE 'CHAIN OF EVIDENCE' IN CASE STUDY ANALYSIS

For her dissertation Professor De Weerd-Nederhof of the University of Twenty studied new product development (NPD) and has since become well published in this area. Her research purpose was to understand and map NPD as a dynamic process within its context. She relied on Yin (1989) for guidance of the process and explains below what she regards as most important: 'In my experience, the most important thing in this type of research is "*netjes werken*", a Dutch expression used, for example, by De Leeuw (1993) in his book on methodology, referring to conscientiousness in data collection; good documentation and issues of awareness, anticipation and perhaps most importantly, traceability (building a chain of evidence)' (De Weerd-Nederhof, 2001, p. 527).

However, such approaches are of limited use if there is no overall research strategy guiding what to look for. Even experienced case researchers may sit on their data for a long time in search of an approach to analyzing the data that helps develop interpretations that will yield an acceptable report for the supervising professor or committee or a high-level publication from a single case study.

Later in his career, author Søndergaard was involved in a study involving multiple senior case researchers. He talked about a frustrating experience while attempting to provide interpretation for the data:

> We had interviewed top people in Arla Foods regarding the post-merger integration process. Our case evidence was primarily insiders' post-event evaluations of the process. We finished the data gathering, but the data did not talk to us beyond developing descriptive categories – until we were brought together with a Dutch and French team of top researchers. They were involved in a much larger case study that focused on the KLM/Air France merger. They had, partly, a similar research design. The use of both sets of information enabled us to use a cross-case synthesis and pattern-finding analysis process (Søndergaard and Noorderhaven, 2016, pp. 9–10).

The overall research strategy of the case study process is highly important to establish the basis on which to conduct a rigorous empirical analysis of case evidence. One issue is certainly having the purpose of the research clearly spelled out. Moving forward required rigorous thinking together with careful consideration of alternative explanations comparing two similar large, successful post-merger integrations of cross-border mergers that were embedded in very different social contexts, which provided a more sufficient presentation of evidence. Another important aspect of the research purpose is whether the research is intended to be descriptive or identify casual relationships, perhaps of a predictive or prescriptive nature.

5.2 How do content analysis and QDAs help case study research?

Some researchers talk about content or thematic analysis of the set of data they have gathered in the course of their case research projects. These researchers are referring to the development of a set of keywords, multi-word phrases, or short sentences that help explain aspects of the data that appear in first, second, and subsequent readings of the data. The researchers may suggest 'tagging', meaning developing a way of indexing or coding the data.

In her project on divestment, author Taylor (1988) undertook a thematic analysis. She drew together all the transcripts of the interviews into one notebook and used tags as she read multiple times through the voluminous set of transcripts. The tags were color coded (inasmuch as there were sufficient colors available!) to keywords that appeared to describe aspects of the phenomena that appeared important. A student assistant then made a copy of all the pages – complete with the tags and penciled notations. The student assistant cut up the transcripts so that the sections of the transcripts were, at first glance, what appeared to be hand-shredded paper! Taylor then organized the 'scraps' into heaps where the words or phrases were related. Each grouping was placed in file folders labeled with the word, words, or phrases chosen to describe the aspect of the phenomenon she had determined the 'scraps' related to. In essence she undertook a thorough content or thematic analysis. From these files she wrote about the themes that emerged from the analysis in her 1988 book on divestment.

Taylor's approach was hand done. In contrast, Carrington and Tayles (2012) used the qualitative data analysis (QDA) program NVivo[2] developed by the Australian-based company QSR International to assist in their content analysis. NVivo can deeply analyze the data using powerful search, query and visualization tools and uncover subtle connections, add insights and ideas as you work, rigorously justify findings, and effortlessly share your work. The two case studies Carrington and Tayles undertook were focused on intellectual capital. Specifically, they wanted to understand how hotel managers used intellectual capital in their decision-making. The data sources were interviews, documentation and materials from the organizations' archives. These authors explained the approach they used with the data:

> [We used] content analysis as the technique for analyzing the multiple sources of evidence. The transcriptions of the interviews, case notes from documentation and archival records were typed and formatted into text files and uploaded into NVivo. This enabled the classification of the information to explore the emerging themes. This was in keeping with the methodological procedure for conducting qualitative content analysis (Kapborg and Berterö, 2003). The text was first read and initial codes emerged that enabled data reduction by flagging up those chunks of text where key themes seemed to recur as suggested (David and Sutton, 2004). Interpretive content analysis was then used to clarify vague, unclear and contradictory sentences. Reports on each initial code identified were produced from textual data through a systematic method of reduction and analysis (Priest et al., 2002). This process resulted in two themes for human capital, three themes for relational capital and three themes for structural capital. These emerging themes were further analyzed in relation to the relevant theories (Carrington and Tayles, 2012, pp. 247–248)

We do want to emphasize that QDAs cannot be utilized until the case study researcher first develops key words and phrases to be utilized in search through the content. These keywords or phrases might be drawn, at least partially, from the existing literature. However, the researcher has a responsibility of also using an interpretivist mode in reading, absorbing, and understanding the accumulated body of research materials in developing these keywords and phrases. We will speak more about the interpretivist approach in the next chapter.

Content analysis is important to understand because of its frequent use. Given the increasing developments in computer technology, use of QDA programs certainly makes sense especially in multi-case studies with a large sample. In such case studies the amount of data appears daunting as the data can take the form of interview transcripts and other supporting materials such as observational notes, company documents, or external publications. Two other examples of the use of QDAs and content analysis appear in Box 5.2.

BOX 5.2

CASE STUDY-BASED RESEARCH THAT USED QSR INTERNATIONAL'S CDA SOFTWARE

Software to assist in the analysis: two examples

Example 1: Parlalis (2011) examined the development of a discharge program in a Scotland-based learning disability hospital. The data was gathered in the form of structured interviews with the interviewees who were identified through a snowball process. Once the interviews were transcribed, Parlalis used QSR NUD*IST (version N6) to undertake the content analysis. The process suggested use of various management models across the four phases of the development process.

Example 2: Gomes and Gomes (2009) used a four-case study design to examine the manner in which Brazilian local authorities made decisions within the constraints of stakeholder presence. The data was in the form of 28 interviews. The content analysis using the QSR N6[a] software identified clusters of stakeholder concerns. The results from the overall study suggested that the *number* of stakeholders exerting pressure is less important than the *kind of influence* the stakeholder (i.e., the recipient of the influence) expected to have on the decision-making process.

Note: a. The company QSR International released its first CAQDAS (Computer Assisted Qualitative Data AnalysiS) program under the name NUDIST. The company released NUDIST as an N series beginning in 1997, and the NVivo series beginning 2002.

5.3 What various forms of data coding relate to case study research?

The QDA software does not automatically produce the themes and constructs embedded in the data. You, as the researcher, have the responsibility for establishing the initial keywords that will guide the software analysis. Part of that aspect of the research strategy is to decide on the approach to analyzing the case evidence. An early stage in the analysis is organizing the data in order to be able to use the analyzing technique. The examples in section 5.2 on content analysis certainly make it clear that data organizing is very important.

A next stage is often coding. Below we outline a three-step approach to develop theory through use of open, axial, and selective (or subjective) coding:

1. *Open coding.* Open coding refers to 'examining, comparing, conceptualizing, and categorizing data' (Strauss and Corbin, 1990, p. 61). The author may or may not approach the coding with or without a priori categories, depending on the purpose. A research project that does not use a priori categories is often referred to as 'grounded theory'. In grounded theory the categories will arise from the data at the coding stage. The researcher is essentially taking on the task of ascertaining how well the data accumulated in the current study demonstrates that the same phenomena are occurring (Gomes and Gomes, 2009). If a priori categories have been established, they were probably drawn from earlier work by the same author or others. Generally, even if the researcher uses a priori categories, additional insights will arise during the analysis process due to the richness or 'thick description' of the data. The line between whether the researcher is using grounded theory or not, is, therefore, never quite clear in case research.

   The researcher should move from the data to categories to groupings or situations providing that categories do arise from this phase of the coding. Once the researcher is satisfied that the categorization is reasonably complete, groupings need to be evaluated/considered in terms of characteristics such as frequency of occurrence, duration, or some other measure that may inform the theory-building aspect of the research.

2. *Axial coding.* Axial coding enables the researcher to develop the relationships among the groupings. In this process the researcher focuses on identifying the logic relationships among the categories of data. The relationships may be longitudinal, tentative causal, or cross-sectional in nature. The logic relationships are usually inferred based on observed

connections among events, reports from interviewees, or characteristics of the interviewees.

3. *Selective (or subjective) coding.* In this phase the researcher is conceptualizing. The development of the theory or at least a series of testable propositions is occurring. The researcher is moving to infer generalization. If the research is confirmatory in nature, the researcher is using the results of the coding to demonstrate affirmation or denial of the validity of an a priori model. This phase of the analysis consists of five steps: (a) developing a storyline or an overarching core category; (b) relating other concepts that were identified with the core category; (c) developing propositions or hypotheses that are the researcher's explanation of the observed relationships between the concepts from step 2 and the overarching category in step 1; (d) refining the storyline to be less technical in its explanation; and (e) relating the propositions or hypotheses to the dimensions observed in the case studies (Stall-Meadows and Hyle, 2010).[3]

5.4 How does Robert Yin suggest we go about analyzing our case study data?

In this section we overview the five approaches Yin suggests for analyzing case evidence, (1) pattern matching; (2) explanation building; (3) time series; (4) logic models; and (5) cross-case synthesis. Pattern matching occurs in all of these approaches, but in different ways and under different conditions. Robert Yin (2009, pp. 127–62) is the main source for this section.

Pattern matching

Pattern matching involves the process of going back and forth from the collected data to what was anticipated. What was anticipated may have been derived from related literature and one way of pattern matching is to make comparisons with 'conflicting literature' and 'similar literature' (De Weerd-Nederhof, 2001).

Overall, pattern matching requires comparing the constructs or theory guiding the research with the data, and considering and reconsidering the analysis and perhaps even collecting additional data. In this sense, matching is one of the foundations on which we undertake the process of interpreting our data (Dubois and Gadde, 2002).[4] If the study has an explanatory purpose, then the patterns can be related to the dependent or the independent variables of the study. If the purpose of the study is descriptive, pattern match is an important technique especially for situations in which a predicted pattern

---

BOX 5.3

FOCUS GROUP PATTERN MATCHING EXAMPLE

Miyauchi and Perry (1999) provide an example of pattern matching for analysis of focus group transcripts. The focus groups were undertaken for the Australian mango industry. These two authors compared the Japanese focus group participants' responses with responses given by Australian consumers. They also compared the consumers' views of fruit characteristics with findings from previous studies.

BOX 5.4

CHIN'S GUIDANCE ON PATTERN MATCHING

Chin (2013, p. 203) argues that 'a pattern matching analysis. . .enables researchers to capture subtle similarities and differences within cases and associate them with a specific pattern, and is believed to further reinforce the systematic application of a multiple-case study (Rialp et al., 2005)'.

Chin points out that multiple cases provide replication and thus can contribute to the reliability of results. He refers to Eisenhardt and Graebner (2007) in arguing that multiple-case research typically yields more robust, generalizable theory than single cases and provides an example of a two-case study that used pattern matching analysis. The design was deliberate and intended to enhance explanatory power.

---

of the specific variables is defined before the data collection takes place (see example applied to a focus group design in Box 5.3 and further guidance in Box 5.4).

The role of the general research strategy is twofold. First, it is to determine the best ways to contrast any differences as sharply as possible. Second, the general research strategy needs to develop theoretically significant explanations for the different outcomes.

Using rival explanations is a useful general analytical strategy. This approach provides a process for pattern matching for dependent and independent variables. Several cases may be known to have a certain type of outcome and the analysis has to focus on how this outcome occurred in each case. This analysis requires the development of rival theoretical propositions. This approach is dialectic in nature as it involves offering alternative explanations to ascertain which one appears to have the best fit.[5]

In some situations, simpler patterns are relevant and more compelling. A simple pattern is having a minimum of dependent and independent variables, perhaps as few as two variables overall.

The pattern matching process does not result in precise comparisons. The actual pattern that is identified may involve no quantitative or statistical criteria. Rather, the results require interpretive discretion on the part of the case study researcher because the low levels of precision do not readily permit statistical analysis. One caution is that the pattern matching process may lead to a case study researcher too readily declaring that a pattern has been matched. On the other hand, a case researcher may be overly restrictive in claiming an expected pattern was violated. Both dangers can be avoided by subjecting the interpretation to discussion with supervisors or colleagues. Yin suggests that pattern matching case study analysis can be made stronger by 'developing more precise measures. In the absence of such precision, an important suggestion is to avoid postulating very subtle patterns, so that your pattern matching deals with gross matches or mismatches whose interpretation is less likely to be challenged' (Yin, 2009, p. 141).

Explanation building

Explanation building is an extension of the pattern matching technique. This process is appropriate to use with case study research that is exploratory in nature. This approach does not start with any predicted patterns. In all likelihood, you are using very open-ended research questions as you interview.

Time series

Time series analysis in simple form consists of assembling key events into a chronology. From one perspective, time series analysis is simpler than general pattern matching analysis, because there may be only one single dependent or independent variable to trace through the data. On the other hand, using a time series process is more complicated, because the starting or ending points of the single variable may not be clear. However, the ability to trace changes in the site or subject over time is a major strength of case study research. One such example is the Campbell study of Connecticut's speed limit law in 1955, which Yin describes (2009, p. 145). Complex time series analyses are useful when the trends within the given case involve multiple variables. The strength of the case study strategy is the potential to develop a rich explanation for the complex pattern of outcomes and in comparing the explanations with outcomes.

Logic models

Logic models deal with complex chains of events over a period of time. The events are staged in repeated cause–effect patterns. An event that is a dependent variable in one phase of the chain of events becomes an independent variable or a causal event for the next phase. Logic models are used as a technique for analyzing the case evidence when the purpose of the case study is evaluation. The use of logic models can also consist of matching an empirically observed event to a theoretically predicted event. As you no doubt noted, the logic model technique is another pattern matching process.

This approach can be used for different levels of the phenomenon under study. Individual-level logic models can be used when your case study is about an individual person. An organizational-level logic model traces events taking place in an organization. Program-level logical models detect the rationale underlying, for instance, social programs, and can be used to organize analyzing data from several case studies.

Cross-case synthesis

Cross-case synthesis is a process used for analyzing case evidence from at least two cases. Before undertaking cross-case comparisons, it is important that we have thoroughly used one or more of the approaches above for a thorough within-case analysis (De Weerd-Nederhof, 2001, p. 517). In this phase of cross-case analysis each individual case study is treated as a separate study. The advantage of the cross-case synthesis is that the analysis is likely to be easier and the findings more robust than relying on a single case analysis. This approach can be carried out as a predesigned part of a multiple-case study project carried out by the same or different researchers.

The cross-case approach may also be used to compare case studies developed as a result of independent case research studies carried out by different researchers. One example is author Søndergaard's serendipitous identification of other researchers who were focusing on a similar phenomenon as occurred in the Arla Foods and KLM/Air France studies (Søndergaard and Noorderhaven, 2016). Bushe and Kassam (2005) took a similar approach in a project that analyzed 20 cases from four-case study research-based dissertations that focused on the application of the appreciative inquiry (AI) process. With a large number of case studies, quantitative techniques or meta-analyses can be used. Author Taylor has been using a more quantitative approach with an ongoing research on born global firms in which she is examining the cases in articles based on case research (Taylor and Yang, 2007; Taylor, Yang,

Coates, and Sphar, 2008; Coates, Sphar, Taylor, and Yang, 2009; Taylor, Coates, Sphar, and Yang, 2009; Taylor and Coates, 2010).

If the sample consists of a small number of cases, a concrete suggestion is to construct a matrix with key words, categories or phrases along one side of the matrix and the cases along the other. The data from the individual cases is entered in the cells. The researcher's examination of word tables to identify cross-case patterns relies on argumentative interpretation. Yin (1989, 2009) reminds us that the case researcher therefore needs to develop strong, plausible and fair arguments that are supported by the data. Such a matrix might initially look like Table 5.1. The phrases or words in each of the cells can then be cross-compared to ascertain similarities and differences and reduced in a second version to words or short phrases.

Taylor's use of file folders to organize the coded sections of cut-up interviews essentially followed a similar process. Anyansi-Archibong in her dissertation process involving nine case studies essentially followed a similar process, although the data matrix eventually covered most of a wall (Anyansi-Archibong, 1985).

In practice, you can use these five techniques in combination for analyzing case evidence. If you do so, be sure to be very clear about the logic of the various processes applied when using the techniques of pattern matching in combination. Doing so is important in order to maintain the transparency of how you reasoned from facts or case events to explanations. De Weerd-Nederhof's admonition in Box 5.1 regarding 'traceability' or 'building a chain of evidence' is critical (2001, p. 527). Others echo this admonition. Seuring (2008) admonishes us to more thoroughly document our case study research processes. His admonition applies regardless of whether we deliver our case study work in a class report, a thesis, a dissertation, or a peer-reviewed journal. Another way of thinking about this matter comes from Lillis and Mundy (2005). They urge the researcher to maintain a clear 'audit trail' of the data-gathering and analysis processes.

A final word is needed in order to understand Yin's suggestions that we describe above. Yin's guidance regarding case study analysis has been rightly described as positivistic in nature (Rowley, 2002). Positivism insists that the researcher objectively gathers and objectively analyzes the data.

Reductionist approaches are also positivistic. Reductionist approaches take the tack of attempting to reduce complex phenomena to their parts and studying those parts in order to attempt to understand those aspects in

Table 5.1 Utilization of researchers' observations or measures in one or more case studies[a]

Variable (or dimension) number	Case number				
	Case #1	Case #2	Case #3		Case #n[b]
#1: Country of origin/ location	Australia	Sweden	New Zealand	. . .	. . .
#2: Country location of first cross-border activity	Germany	Germany	USA	. . .	. . .
#3: Type of technology	CAD developer of retail design for photo/pharmacy outlets	Monoleaflet heart valve	High-tech voice activated electronics	. . .	. . .
#4: Code for technology[c]	Hi	Very hi	Hi	. . .	. . .
#5: . . .	. . .	. . .	. . .	. . .	. . .
#r:[d] . . .	. . .	. . .	. . .	. . .	. . .

Notes:
a. For simplicity we have included simple categories such as country of origin/location and country location of first cross-border activity. For variable or dimension #3 the data in the cell for type of technology generally drew on multiple statements. The researchers summarized the description and then designated a code. They undertook the coding separately and then compared notes. If they disagreed, they discussed the technology related to a particular case and resolved differences. Within each cell the researcher enters the observation or measurement regarding this variable or dimension in the particular case. We use 'observation' to mean qualitative information and 'measure' to mean a quantitative representation of the information. The simple example above refers to an analysis undertaken by the born global research team (Coates et al., 2009).
b. N is the size of the sample – that is, the number of cases or units drawn from the case study research publications that are used as the sample.
c. In this chapter we mentioned the ongoing research on the born global phenomenon by author Taylor and colleague Coates. For the technology aspect of each case study the researchers independently coded the technology of the firms. Such an approach can provide a check regarding the reliability of the coding
d. The research by author Taylor et al. involves case studies summarized in over 50 articles and numerous variables or dimensions.

more depth. Some approaches to case study analysis do attempt to do so. They border on the more quantitative approaches to qualitative research in general. Coding and counting, simply put, is reductionist. But, the case study researcher simultaneously focuses on understanding the whole – that is, the systems perspective of understanding the unit of analysis *and* its context. In this role as a researcher you are taking an 'interpretivist' approach, a matter that we will explore further in the next chapter.

5.5   Concluding remarks

In this chapter we have considered approaches to analyzing the data accumulated in the course of the research. We started with asking why there is often a delay between data gathering and completing data analysis, citing author Søndergaard's frustrating experiences. Then we looked at content analysis, as every other approach we describe harkens back to this basic process in helping to understand the basic patterns in the data. In our third section we examined three approaches to coding – open, axial, and selective. Coding helps us to understand what goes on in the phenomenon and permits us to move to a level of abstraction that potentially allows us to make sense of the patterns in the data. In the fourth section we examined Yin's suggested approaches, which help us to make those generalizations from our data.

The case study methodology will most likely continue to garner and, often, to merit criticism. However, no less so than the work of our more quantitatively oriented colleagues. Those of us who utilize more qualitative methods such as case study research must, at the very least, follow the advice of our colleagues to clearly explain and document our entire process. Yin and other researchers hold us to that standard – and even more we must hold ourselves to it.

 END OF CHAPTER QUESTIONS AND ANSWERS

1 **Why is there often a delay between data gathering and completion of data analysis?** The choice of process of analyzing the data collected in the case study project is often, perhaps, unnecessarily postponed. Prior to the data analysis, there are a number of issues that need attention. These include challenges such as developing research questions, data collection design and getting access. There is well-developed and detailed guidance about handling these processes. However, little such guidance exists regarding the analysis of the data. We suggest that part of the point of departure for a rigorous empirical analysis of case evidence is to have the purpose of the research clearly spelled out, for instance whether the research is intended to be descriptive, identify causal relations or aiming at a predictive or prescriptive purpose.

2 **How do content analysis and QDAs help case study research?** Content analysis by developing a set of keywords, multi-word phrases, or short sentences help explain aspects of the data that appear in first, second, and subsequent data readings and 'tagging', meaning developing a way of indexing or coding the data. To assist in content analysis, qualitative data analysis (QDA) such as NVivo can be used. NVivo, for instance, deeply analyzes data using powerful search, query and visualization tools that can uncover subtle connections. We suggest that it makes sense to use QDA programs in multi-case studies with a large sample, with multi-type data sources in the form of interview transcripts and other supporting materials such as observational notes, company documents, or external publications. Still, the researcher needs to make keywords and phrases to use to search through the content *before* QDAs will be used.

3 **What various forms of data coding relate to case study research?** In this chapter we outline a three-step approach to developing theory through the use of open, axial, and subjective

coding. (1) Open coding refers to examining, comparing, conceptualizing, and categorizing data. The coding is approached with or without a priori categories, depending on the purpose. Open coding ascertains how well the data accumulated in the current study demonstrates that the same phenomena are occurring. (2) Axial coding helps the researcher to develop the relationships among the groupings with a focus on identifying the logic relationships among the categories of data. Logic relationships are inferred from observed connections among events, reports from interviewees, or the interviewees' characteristics. (3) Subjective coding or selective coding is about conceptualizing – the researcher is moving to infer generalization. The development of the theory or at least a series of testable propositions is occurring. The results of the coding are used to demonstrate affirmation of or denial of the validity of an a priori model, if the research is confirmatory. This phase of the analysis consists of five steps: (a) developing a storyline or an overarching core category, (b) relating other concepts that were identified with the core category, (c) developing propositions or hypotheses that are the researcher's explanation of the observed relationships between the concepts from step 2 and the overarching category in step 1, (d) refining the storyline to be less technical in its explanation and (e) relating the propositions or hypotheses to the dimensions observed in the case studies.

4   **How does Yin suggest we go about analyzing our case study data?** Yin suggests five approaches to analyzing case evidence: (a) pattern matching; (b) explanation building; (c) time series; (d) logic models; and (e) cross-case synthesis.

NOTES

1   Indeed, Yin (2009) underscores the neglect of analysis very bluntly when he says: 'Too many times, investigators start case studies without having the foggiest notion about how the evidence is to be analyzed' (p. 127).

2   QSR International's first software product was NU*DIST (or NUDIST). The company later introduced its N series and then the NVivo series. These programs are variously referred to as computer-assisted qualitative data analysis software (CAQDAS) or qualitative data (QDA) programs. These programs have multiple competitors available from other competitors and as freeware. The CAQDAS assist with content analysis. Guthrie and Abeysekera (2006) suggest that '[t]he basic technique of content analysis is an observational research method used to systematically evaluate the symbolic content of all forms of communication (Kolbe and Burnett, 1991). It provides scientific, objective, quantitative and generalizable description of content analysis. It can be used on virtually any medium with verbal and/or visual content – printed material, radio and television programmes, recorded movies, readings, songs, etc. It has been extensively used in marketing and consumer behavior research (Kassarjian, 1997; Wheeler, 1998; Sayre, 1992; Guthrie and Abeysekera, 2006)... The basic technique of content analysis consists of counting the number of times pre-defined categories of measurement appear in a given content' (Guthrie and Abeysekera, 2006, p. 120; see also Kolbe and Burnett, 1991; Sayre, 1992; Kassarjian, 1977; Wheeler, 1998). Tom and Linda Richards, co-founders of QSR, caution that before utilizing a QDA program the researcher must first read and become acquainted with the data (Richards and Richards, 2004).

3   Stall-Meadows and Hyle (2010) explained how they utilized their three-step process. Their data were four dissertations that utilized case study methodology. They chose the four from a list of 18 that focused on teaching attitudes and actions. Note that these authors do an efficient job of explaining the grounded theory process (but, their five-step process is a bit murky). They suggest that if the hypotheses are supported by the data in over half the cases, the hypotheses can then be extracted. Hypotheses (Strauss and Corbin, 1990) must be written as statements using the format: under these conditions, this happens; whereas, under these conditions, this happens.

4   Dubois and Gadde (2002) used a single-case research design that was aimed at theory development.

5   A humorous example of this approach occurs in almost every episode of the USA comedy-mystery series *Castle*. The mystery writer Castle is the partner to well-respected (and beautiful) Detective Beckett. Frequently, as the case unfolds, Castle will quickly present two or three propositions or hypotheses of why the crime may have occurred and (thus) 'whodunit'. Although his suggested explanations are frequently

shot down, Castle is always a valuable asset in solving the murder mystery. His deduction is juxtapositioned in the series against the careful data gathering by Detective Beckett's team and their, often ponderous, examination of the accumulating evidence.

REFERENCES

Anyansi-Archibong, C.B. (1985), 'Evolution of firms: Strategy and structure of enterprise in a third world country', dissertation, University of Kansas.

Bushe, G.R. and A.F. Kassam (2005), 'When is appreciative inquiry transformational? A meta-case analysis', *The Journal of Applied Behavioral Science*, **41**(2), 161–81.

Carrington, D. and M. Tayles (2012), 'Intellectual capital in the Caribbean hospitality industry: Two qualitative case studies', *The Electronic Journal of Knowledge Management*, **10**(3), 244–57.

Chin (2013), 'An exploratory study on upgrading by FDI OEMs in China', *International Business Research*, **6**(1), 199–210.

Coates, T., A. Sphar, M. Taylor, and X. Yang (2009), 'Born global firms: A meta-analysis of cases in the literature', *Proceedings*, Administrative Sciences Association of Canada.

David, M. and C.D. Sutton (2004), *Social Research. The Basics*, Thousand Oaks, CA: Sage.

De Leeuw, A.C.J. (1993), *Een boekje over bedrijfskundige methodologie: Management van onderzoek [Business Management Methodology: Management Research]*, 2nd edition, Assen/Maastricht: Van Gorcum.

De Weerd-Nederhof, P.C. (2001), 'Qualitative case study research. The case of a PhD research project on organising and managing new product development systems', *Management Decision*, **39**(7), 513–38.

Dubois, A. and L.-E. Gadde (2002), 'Systematic combining: An abductive approach to case research', *Journal of Business Research*, **55**(7), 553–60.

Eisenhardt, K.M. and M.E. Graebner (2007), 'Theory building from cases: Opportunities and challenges', *Academy of Management Journal*, **50**(1), 25–32.

Gomes, R.C. and L. de Oliveira Miranda Gomes (2009), 'Depicting the arena in which Brazilian local government authorities make decisions', *International Journal of Public Sector Management*, **22**(2), 76–90.

Guthrie, J. and I. Abeysekera (2006), 'Content analysis of social, environmental reporting: What is new?' *Journal of Human Resource Costing and Accounting*, **10**(2), 114–26.

Kapborg, I. and C. Berterö (2003), 'The phenomenon of caring from the novice student nurse's perspective: A qualitative content analysis', *International Nursing Review*, **50**(3), 183–92.

Kassarjian, H.H. (1977), 'Content analysis in consumer research', *Journal of Consumer Research*, **4**(1), 8–18.

Kolbe, R.H. and M.S. Burnett (1991), 'Content analysis research. An examination of applications with directives for improving reliability and objectivity', *Journal of Consumer Research*, **18**(2), 243–50.

Lillis, A.M. and J. Mundy (2005), 'Cross-sectional field studies in management accounting research – closing the gaps between surveys and case-studies', *Journal of Management Accounting Research*, **17**(1), 119–44.

Miyauchi, Y. and C. Perry (1999), 'Marketing fresh fruit to Japanese consumers: Exploring issues for Australian exporters', *European Journal of Marketing*, **33**(1/2), 196–205.

Parlalis, S. (2011), 'Management of organizational changes in a case of de-institutionalization', *Journal of Health Organization and Management*, **25**(4), 355–84.

Priest, H., P. Roberts, and L. Woods (2002), 'An overview of three different approaches to the interpretation of qualitative data', *Nurse Researcher*, **10**(1), 30–51.

Rialp, A., J. Rialp, D. Urbano, and Y. Vaillant (2005), 'The born-global phenomenon: A comparative case study research', **3**(2), 133–71.

Richards, L. and T. Richards (2004), Tools and methods: using and teaching NVivo and N6 in different methodological contexts, Sept., accessed 31 March 2017 at https://www.surrey.ac.uk/sociology/research/researchcentres/caqdas/files/QSRSept04.pdf.

Rowley, J. (2002), 'Using case studies in research', *Management Research News*, **25**(1), 116–27.

Sayre, S. (1992), 'Content analysis as a tool for consumer research', *Journal of Consumer Marketing*, **9**(1), 15–25.

Seuring, S.A. (2008), 'Assessing the rigor of case study research in supply chain management', *Supply Chain Management,* **13**(2), 128–37.

Søndergaard, M. (1990), 'På Sporet af den nationale kulturs konsekvenser, En sammenligning af praksis i danske og franske pengeinstitutetter, den nationale kulturs betydning' [In search of national cultures' consequences. A comparison of practices in Danish and French banks, the significance of national culture], unpublished PhD thesis, Aarhus Business School.

Søndergaard, M. and N. Noorderhaven (2016), 'Stakeholder management in cross border mergers', conference paper, Meeting of Academy of International Business, New Orleans.

Stall-Meadows, C. and A. Hyle (2010), 'Procedural methodology for a grounded meta-analysis of qualitative case studies', *International Journal of Consumer Studies,* **34**(4), 412–18.

Strauss, A. and J. Corbin (1990), *Basics of Qualitative Research, Techniques and Procedures for Developing Grounded Theory*, 2nd edition, Thousand Oaks, CA: Sage.

Taylor, M.L. (1988), *Divesting Business Units – Making the Decision and Making it Work*, Lexington, MA: Lexington Books.

Taylor, M. and T. Coates (2010), 'SnowSports and the born global research project', presentation at the 'Using Cases to Build Theory' Professional Development Workshop, Academy of Management, August, 2010, Montreal.

Taylor, M. and X. Yang (2007), 'SnowSports Interactive – the dilemmas of being born global', *North American Case Research Association Proceedings*, Keystone, CO, October 18–20.

Taylor, M., T. Coates, A. Sphar, and X. Yang (2009), 'Understanding born globals in 12 countries: The influence of technology on Hofstede distance measures', Midwest Academy of Management, St. Louis, MO.

Taylor, M., A. Yang, T. Coates, and A. Sphar (2008), 'Born global companies: A preliminary multi-country analysis', Midwest Academy of Management, St. Louis, MO.

Watts, M. (2007), 'They have tied me to a stake: Reflections on the art of case study research', *Qualitative Inquiry,* **13**(2), 204–17.

Wheeler, D.R. (1998), 'Content analysis an analytical technique for international marketing research', *International Marketing Review,* **5**(4), 35–40.

Yin, R.K. (1989), *Case Study Research: Design and Methods*, revised edition, Thousand Oaks, CA: Sage.

Yin, R.K. (2009), *Case Study Research: Design and Methods*, 4th edition, Thousand Oaks, CA: Sage.

6

Theory, abductive reasoning, and interpretivism

 LEARNING OBJECTIVES

The chapter addresses three questions:

1 How do descriptive, predictive, and prescriptive theory relate to case study research?

2 Why is abductive reasoning important for a case researcher to understand?

3 What does an interpretivist approach have to do with case study research?

As we come toward the end of this book on case study methodology, we realize there is much more we could cover. However, in this penultimate chapter we introduce additional ideas to help you with your case research study. Before moving to our final chapter in which we summarize 18 capsules that we believe you need to remember when undertaking a case study project, let's examine the three questions above.

6.1 How do descriptive, predictive, and prescriptive theory relate to case study research?[1]

In this section we first describe descriptive, predictive, and prescriptive theory. Second, we consider how they are interrelated. Third, we discuss how they are related to case study research.

Descriptive theory

Descriptive theory does just exactly what the name suggests – it describes what was at the time of observation. Generally, but not always, a case study project aimed at descriptive theory will focus on only one case, that is, a sample of one. In Box 6.1, 'Action Research – An MBA Team in Action', Phase Two describes the development of a descriptive model, or theory, of the new product development (NPD) program at TCC (Terra Chemical Company).

Case research methodology is often aimed at developing descriptive theory. The descriptive theory or model may be the baseline for undertaking a more extensive study – or, it may be the purpose of the study. For example, Porporato (2009) undertook a study to provide a description of the implementation of management control systems (MCS) in two joint ventures (JVs) in the automobile industry. She made her purpose clear when she stated: 'The main purpose of this study is to describe the sequence in which MCS are initially implemented in JVs' and 'The purpose of this paper and case studies of JVs in the motor and auto parts industry is to describe and explain the sequence of MCS implementation in JVs'. She described her research as 'novel' (Porporato, 2009, p. 271), meaning that few or no research projects had looked at this phenomenon. She utilized the argument that a descriptive study was important, given there had not been any previous documented evidence of the particular phenomenon. Another example of a longitudinal study was carried out by Klakegg, Torp, and Austeng (2010) where the authors succinctly summarize the tension between the developing systems that are judged to have rigor and are, yet, simple to understand.[2]

What do descriptive case studies or descriptive theory achieve for us? They help us understand. As demonstrated in the work of the MBA team with TCC in Box 6.1, the description provided a baseline. The descriptive case study may also provide insights into the mindsets of the individuals who are actors in the organization we are studying or the individuals who are our unit of analysis (Thatcher, 2006).[3]

During the process of the research we gather data about the phenomenon we want to study. If we study the phenomenon in other settings, we also investigate whether the same relationships are observed in the other settings. The research stream can proceed toward prediction and ultimately prescription, if the data supports the descriptive theory. We need to remember, however, that supporting or affirming a theory does not 'prove' it. If, for example, researchers find that there are 'oddballs' or anomalies in the results, they either delve into that aspect of the phenomenon themselves or encourage others to do so. More intensive scrutiny and follow-on research can move a theory forward. Kuhn, one of our most influential philosophers of science in the twentieth century, makes this issue abundantly clear in his classic work *The Structure of Scientific Revolutions* (1962).

BOX 6.1

ACTION RESEARCH – AN MBA TEAM IN ACTION

In Fall 2013, a team of MBA students in author Taylor's class undertook a consulting project to help Terra Chemical Company, Inc. (TCC) improve its new product development (NPD) process. The project consisted of four phases, which are outlined below:

Phase One: The students read articles about the NPD process. From their readings as well as from their conversations with their gatekeeper or project sponsor, the Executive VP of the company, they developed an interview protocol that they used in the second phase.

Phase Two: At the beginning of this phase, two members of the team conducted an informal group interview with TCC's executives. The informal group interview included participant observation as the two team members were invited to the company's annual picnic. During the meal they sat at a table with members of the executive team. Following the picnic, the total group of TCC executives held a meeting in which the two MBA students were invited to participate. Part of the executive agenda was to talk as a group about the NPD process. The MBA team members later conducted individual interviews with all the members of the top executive team and some of the people who reported to the executives. Two members of the MBA team conducted each interview. One led the questions. The other concentrated on making notes. The team also recorded the interviews. Because time was limited, the MBA team did not transcribe the interviews, but all of the MBA team members did review all of the notes and recordings. From the data from Phase One and Phase Two the team developed a model that described the current NPD process at TCC.

Phase Three: The team undertook to compare the TCC's NPD process with the literature they had read on effective NPD processes. They also talked with a faculty member from their own university and another faculty member from a second university. Both of the faculty members were known to have insights about NPD processes. As the project progressed, the team also kept very close contact with the project sponsor from TCC. The executives who had been interviewed all reported to the sponsor. He, in turn, reported to the president and board. The members of the team also interacted with the other members of the executive team via telephone. As Phase Three progressed, the MBA team designed a revised NPD process with specific recommendations and a recommended timeline for implementation of TCC's new NPD process.

Phase Four: The MBA team made a presentation before TCC's executive team, a set of executives from the business community, and the other members of the MBA class. There was lively discussion among all participants.

Readers might be interested to know that the judges and executives commended the work of the team. Further, the executive vice-president sent several e-mails over the next month

➡

←

indicating how the firm had begun to implement the recommendations from the consulting project.

Because of the restrictions of the semester and course content, the team had only about nine weeks to work on the project. Necessarily there was some truncation of what would have been an ideal research process. For example, the literature search was not as thorough as it would have been if the time frame had been longer. Further, the interviews were not transcribed and carefully analyzed using a content analysis and coding process. Nonetheless the project as a whole followed approximately the early steps in an action research design that combined (a) descriptive research with the intent of providing (b) prescription. The quality of what the MBA student team did within the time constraints was very high – and the grade that author Taylor rendered after consultation with the client evidenced her commendation and his as well.

Moving a theory forward also involves honing the categorization schemes, improving the variable definitions, and adjusting the measurement systems utilized. Chapter 5 focused on the analysis of the case study evidence and considered interpretivist approaches to data analysis as well as more reductionist-oriented approaches such as the advice of Yin and other authors. The process has echoes of the positivistic direction and bears with it the challenge for the case study researcher to retain a holistic perspective even while keeping the analysis process as systematic and transparent as possible. The challenge is not trivial.

Predictive theory

In predictive theory, the researchers must state the likelihood of outcome(s) under certain conditions. Another way of expressing this notion is that outcomes are contingent upon identified sets of circumstances and some as-yet unidentified circumstances. In multiple regression approaches used with quantitative data, we use the terms 'unexplained variance' or 'error terms'.

These observations also suggest that in order to ascertain causality, it is not enough for researchers to identify multiple instances where the desired outcomes occurred. The research design using such a 'sample' may well demonstrate a common set of characteristics in, for example, successful companies. However, the researcher could not infer causality between the common set of characteristics and success unless the researcher also examined instances in which the desired outcomes did not occur in order to ascertain which of the common set of characteristics were lacking. Only if the common set of characteristics did NOT occur in those organizations where success was not forthcoming, could the researcher draw the conclusion that the specified characteristics were associated with success. There is considerable criticism of the research design when researchers attempt to draw definitive conclusions from a sample of exemplar organizations such as occur in many popular practitioner-oriented books for managers (Christensen and Carlile, 2009, pp. 244–5). Christensen and Carlile's argument regarding this issue implicitly provides significant critique of some very popular works such as *In Search of Excellence* by Peters and Waterman (1982).

Prescriptive theory

Prescriptive theory provides guidance for those of us in the field of practice. It takes the form of advising practitioners on the action to take because a certain outcome or outcomes is likely to occur. Prescriptive theory building follows essentially the same steps as descriptive theory building. That is, in step #1, the researcher collects data by observing, describing, and, perhaps also measuring the phenomena; step #2 categorizes the data often based on *a priori* categorizations that either the researcher or a fellow pursuer of truth utilized in prior research; step #3 analyzes the relationships among those categories with particular attention to the outcome data or variables of interest; and step #4 provides interpretation of inferred causality. However, the process is not as linear as the text may suggest, as researchers move back and forth among the steps.

Prescriptive theory is a form of predictive theory, but it is predictive theory targeted at the practitioner and providing guidance. The MBA project described earlier in Box 6.1 certainly involved a prescriptive component since the project was consultative in nature and its purpose was to provide recommendations – an objective achieved in Phases Three and Four.

Development of predictive and prescriptive theory must include (1) independent and dependent relationships and (2) (thus) at least inference of causality. Well-respected theorists and researchers argue that the usefulness of a theory is its ability to provide guidance to action because it is able to predict with reasonable reliability the expected outcome of the action (Van de Ven, 1989; Bazerman, 2005). Their arguments underscore that prescriptive theory must first have explanatory power – it must be able to show us how under specified circumstances certain outcomes will occur. Second it must pertain to action that will make a difference in the phenomenon and its setting.

How are descriptive, predictive, and prescriptive theory related?

In case study research all three consider an actor, set of actors or a phenomenon within a context. All have dimensions or what in more reductionist mode we refer to as 'variables'. However, whereas descriptive theory will provide an explanation of that unit or analysis and its setting, predictive and prescriptive theory move to separate the aspects of the phenomenon into independent dimensions and dependent dimensions or outcome variables. In so doing they (thus) have at least inference of causality. The premise is that if you can predict outcomes you can move to prescribe action.

Generally, theory development progresses from descriptive to predictive to prescriptive theory. What we mean is that a research stream over time first presents descriptions of the phenomena, which are anchored in observations of those phenomena. The research may lead to predictions about what might happen if aspects of the phenomena were to change or be changed. In prescriptive theory, as Bauer,[4] De Sola Pool, and Dexter (1963) put it, the researcher is attempting to identify the 'leverage points' or levers in the situation in order to give guidance to practitioners as to how to influence the system toward the desired ends.[5] The predictions may emanate from speculations based on one case or inferences based on observations of multiple units, multiple time points within unit, or dynamic observations involving both multiple units and multiple time points. In Table 3.1 and in the appendix tables 3A.1a and 3A.1b in Chapter 3 these research designs are illustrated.

Why is it important to understand the commonalities and differences?

Part of the answer to the question we posed rests on our personal preferences of what we want to attempt to do. But objectively speaking, a great deal relates to the research design choices we make for our case study project. Earlier chapters have covered many of these.

Can we use one case study for descriptive, predictive, or prescriptive purposes?

A study using one case study of one unit of analysis at one period of time will not permit such associational observations. A case that focuses on the phenomenon at one time is acceptable for descriptive purposes only and may be useful for establishing a baseline of understanding about a particular phenomenon. However, a design using two or more case studies or a design investigating the unit of analysis across longitudinal periods can develop associations (Millward and Lewis, 2005).

Can we study one case and make claims about other similar instances? Another way of asking the same question is whether we can generalize from one case? Some argue 'Yes' – for example, Grünbaum (2007, p. 87).[6] Others argue 'No' – for example, Gerring (2004, p. 344).[7] To answer that question requires us to revisit the issues related to differences between the inductive and deductive processes of reasoning. The answer depends on which of the principles of reasoning you are inclined to use. Understanding the difference between inductive and deductive approaches becomes especially important in how we structure the design of our research project. In Chapter 3, we focused on research design and asked questions such as, how many cases are needed? Here we ask, how many cases are included in a research program or project before it is *not* 'case research' (Eisenhardt, 1989)?[8]

As we suggested in Chapter 3, if a research design incorporates one case study, your conclusions are 'speculative'. The one-case study results can be provided as a report on, for example, a particular company at a particular point in time. Whether the situation is typical of other companies at other times or even that company at another point in time is a valid question.

If you are asked, for example, to study an exemplar project within your company to identify guidelines for other similar projects, you are undertaking prescriptive research. However, you must be cognizant that you will no doubt start with description, and then move to prediction by noting the aspects of the project that appeared to be connected with the success, and finally attempt generalizing by suggesting guidelines that other projects might follow.

Predictive observations may lead to prescriptive advice – what management should do to (hopefully!) improve the situation toward greater effectiveness or efficiency. Indeed, to pursue targeted outcomes, a research stream should ultimately provide management with prescriptive theory. But, both predictive and prescriptive theory must be anchored in the descriptive phase of developing theory. The descriptive phase is generally, but not always, associated with qualitative research that is frequently of a case study nature. These three phases of theory development might be carried out by the same researcher or by different researchers over time.

6.2   Why is abductive reasoning important for a case researcher to understand?

In thinking about any kind of research, we must consider the reasoning process that leads to our inferences or conclusions. In Chapter 3 we discussed the two most frequently identified: inductive and deductive. Below we discuss a third, abductive, which is receiving increasing attention and is particularly useful for case research methodology.

The reasoning process underlies the interpretative process. Those processes are very much related to the overall research strategy. The strategy and its components must be matched to how we undertake to understand our data. For data analysis we can, on one hand, use a thematic analysis, as is more frequently used in ethnography. On the other, we can use a more reductionist approach suggested by coding or Yin's five approaches (Yin, 2009) (see Chapter 5). However, 'just' having the analysis is not enough. As case researchers we must then interpret the results of our pattern matching, explanation building, time series, logic models, cross-case synthesis, or thematic analyses. The interpretations require use of creative interpretative processes. Creative processes involve drawing overall inferences or conclusions. The abductive reasoning process will be used here to illustrate how the creative process might work.

The three different ways of reasoning – deductive, inductive, and abductive – differ in distinct ways. In comparison to deductive and inductive reasoning, abduction is the least transparent process. Table 6.1 provides a comparative explanation of the three reasoning processes. Abduction does not follow strict rules of reasoning as induction or deduction do. It has an element of creative reasoning. However, abductive reasoning is used alongside deductive and inductive reasoning (Anderson, 1987).[9]

In abductive reasoning, theories are considered 'versions of the world' (Flick, 2006). In a similar sense Allison (1971) and Allison and Zelikow (1999)[10] suggested three very different models to characterize decision-making observed in the 1962 Cuban Missile Crisis.[11] In abductive reasoning, theories are considered to be much more preliminary, open to questioning, criticizing, rejection, and reshaping on encountering additional empirical data than they are in deductive reasoning (Kelle, 2005; Flick, 2006).

Finnish case study researcher Teea Mäkelä (2013) used abductive reasoning in her study of innovation in a biotechnology firm (see Box 6.2). Mäkelä explained that abductive reasoning differs from inductive

Table 6.1 Comparison of deductive, inductive, and abductive reasoning

Type of reasoning	Explanation
Deductive: the conclusion is, more or less, guaranteed	Deduction is a linear reasoning process in which the logic moves from general theory to specific concrete empirical data or phenomena. Deductive reasoning moves from the general rule to the specific application. Deductive reasoning can assert with a certain degree of certainty the conclusion that is made
Inductive: the conclusion is not as certain, but merely likely	Induction is also a linear process of thinking, but this logic process moves from specific concrete data or phenomena to general theory. Inductive reasoning moves from the specific to the general. Inductive reasoning begins with observations that are specific and limited in scope, and proceeds to a generalized conclusion that is likely, but not certain, in light of accumulated evidence
Abductive: the conclusion arises from taking your best shot	Abduction is a non-linear process of thinking that goes back and forth between general theory and specific data or phenomena (Carcary, 2010). Abductive reasoning typically begins with an incomplete set of observations and proceeds to the likeliest possible explanation for the set. Abductive reasoning is evident in daily decision-making that does its best with the information at hand. That set of information is often incomplete. A medical diagnosis is an application of abductive reasoning. The medical practitioner asks: 'Given this set of symptoms, what is the diagnosis that would best explain most of them?' Its originator, Charles Sanders Peirce (Anderson, 1987), termed abductive 'guessing'. It is used in many business fields including organizational research (Agar, 2010); strategic management (Dew, 2007); entrepreneurship (Freeman, Hutchings, and Chetty, 2012); human resources (Gold, Walton, Cureton, and Anderson, 2011); logistics (Shah, Goldstein, Unger, and Henry, 2008); accounting (Tarr and Mack, 2013); and marketing (Visconti, 2010)

Source: Adapted from Butte College (n.d.), 'TIP Sheet: Deductive, inductive, and abductive reasoning', accessed 7 March 2017 at http://butte.edu/departments/cas/tipsheets/thinking/reasoning.html.

reasoning in that it emphasizes theoretical sensitivity created by an in-depth understanding of possible relevant material. In abductive reasoning, in contrast with inductive reasoning, the researcher does not approach the empirical study as a clean slate or *tabula rasa* but instead uses the existing literature to establish a baseline (see Phase One of the MBA project in Box 6.1). Using abductive reasoning where she utilized findings from previous research made it possible for Mäkelä (2013) to carry out a case study that resulted in innovative new knowledge, a result that would not have been possible using either a deductive or an inductive approach.

BOX 6.2

MÄKELÄ'S DESCRIPTION OF ABDUCTIVE REASONING

To the question, 'In what concrete way was abductive reasoning used?', Mäkelä answered: 'The most concrete example is the constant comparison and theoretical sampling method (of grounded theory). Here, I used literature to constantly focus my attention on items of importance that were coming up in interviews, compare the emerging findings with literature, and guide subsequent data gathering. This, I think, possibly best illustrates how I used literature – as providing background guidance to figure out what I should ask at the interviews, what emerging themes could be new and important and should therefore be followed to a greater extent, and to also analyze the data in that way, as informed by literature but not being limited by it. In concrete terms, in deductive reasoning you start with theory. In inductive reasoning you start with empirical data. In abductive reasoning, you start with both theory and empirical data simultaneously and go back and forth between theory and data'.

Source: E-mail exchanges with author Søndergaard, November 1, 4, 6, 2013.

Abductive reasoning offers powerful tools for research, although it does require significant creative reasoning on the part of the researcher. It may be summarized as a reasoning strategy that modifies and combines elements of previous knowledge and integrates them with new experience (Anderson, 1987; Paavola, 2004). It aims at the creation of new knowledge by combining 'something old and something hitherto unknown' (Peirce, 1903 [1998]). According to Mäkelä (2013), abductive reasoning can be most closely identified with the philosophy of classical pragmatism (Corbin and Strauss, 1990; McDermid, 2006). Classical pragmatism is based on the principle of the need for ideas to be useful, workable and practical.

Abductive reasoning approaches are often used in crime stories or mysteries because of the suspense that occurs when a main character announces the finding of patterns between what have hitherto appeared to be unrelated or trivial events. Dan Brown's mystery novel *The Da Vinci Code* and Umberto Eco's historical murder mystery *The Name of the Rose* certainly use abductive reasoning. But the mastery of the use of abductive reasoning in mystery literature occurs in Sir Arthur Conan Doyle's Sherlock Holmes stories. Below is what Sherlock Holmes refers to as 'reasoning backwards' (BBC News, 2012), a process of pattern matching backwards in time. Sherlock Holmes explains:

> In solving a problem of this sort, the grand thing is to be able to reason backwards. That is a very useful accomplishment, and a very easy one, but people do not practice it much. In the every-day affairs of life it is more useful to reason forwards, and

so the other comes to be neglected. There are fifty who can reason synthetically for one who reason can analytically. . . Let me see if I can make it clearer. Most people, if you describe a train of events to them, will tell you what the result would be. They can put those events together in their minds, and argue from them that something will come to pass. There are few people, however, who, if you told them a result, would be able to evolve from their own inner consciousness what the steps were which led up to that result. This power is what I mean when I talk of reasoning backwards, or analytically (Sherlock Holmes, Chapter 7, 'Conclusion', *A Study in Scarlet*).

Unfolding the mystery of case research involves reasoning based on the pattern-matching techniques outlined above. Part of the process in finding the logic of 'what might be' is using abductive reasoning (e.g., Leavy, 2010). Holmes's backward reasoning is an example of the abductive reasoning process. Holmes, as with any researcher using abductive reasoning, cannot offer certainty or precise assessment of probability, only the best available account of events. This kind of reasoning does not follow strict rules. If you move from the facts to an explanation by process of elimination, you are doing what Holmes calls 'reasoning backwards' (BBC News, 2012). Sherlock puts it very simply below:

There is nothing like first-hand evidence (*A Study in Scarlet*).

The world is full of obvious things which nobody by any chance ever observes (*The Hound of the Baskervilles*).

Eliminate all other factors, and the one which remains must be the truth (*The Sign of Four*).

How often have I said to you that when you have eliminated the impossible, whatever remains, however improbable, must be the truth? (*The Sign of Four*)

Holmes's creative imagination comes up with hypotheses that he tests one by one to see how they fit the data at hand. His logic process is also inductive in nature as his reasoning moves from the specific data to the hypotheses. It is a particular kind of hypothetical reasoning (Eshghi, 1988) that when combined with creative judgment has elements of the garbage-can theory (Cohen, March, and Olsen, 1972).[12] It is also bricolage or, in the more vernacular, tinkering, in that it involves putting together seemingly trivial events to form a pattern.[13] A very simple analogy is a process of 'connecting the dots', of seeing the overarching patterns among the components of the evidence, and coming to that great 'Ah ha!'. In this sense the case researcher is a Sherlock Holmes not only in the matching process but also in explaining critical events.

There are caveats, however. Blaikie (1993) has pointed out that both inductive and deductive forms of research are pure models that do not in fact exist. He proposed a third – 'abductive reasoning' – noting that in this type of reasoning theory, data generation and data analysis are developed simultaneously in a dialectical process. Our own experiences lead us to conclude that while the inductive method does allow the development of new theory, phenomenology cannot take place in a vacuum and current theory must influence the development of categories.

6.3 What does an interpretivist approach have to do with case study research?

The answer to this question is both simple and complex. The simple answer is that case researchers tend to operate on interpretivists' premises. To understand the interpretivist perspective we must compare it to positivistic perspective since interpretivists are referred to as anti-positivists.

Interpretivists view the social world as involving multiple perspectives, subjective realities that are influenced by the values, past experiences, and personal philosophies of the actors in the phenomenon. Interpretivists see the world as messy and complex, not readily reducible to measureable components. Indeed, interpretivists recognize multiple realities related to the same phenomenon. Because interpretivists view the world as complex and largely unpredictable, they tend not to enter into a research project with a fixed design. Indeed, they are often open to an emergent design. The interpretivists' perspective lends itself to case research as case research focuses on capturing the complexity of phenomena. It does so through thick description by including often richly described contexts within which the phenomenon under study is embedded. To the interpretivist it is necessary to become close to and be with the phenomenon under study in order to develop the understanding of the subjective reality of the actors therein.

The interpretivist perspective has long been utilized in management. Organizational theorist Karl Weick (1995, 2001) talked about actors in any situation as processing information and reacting to it. Other theorists have moved one step further by arguing that actors 'enact' their environments. The actors do so through their responses and the influence of those responses on their environment. Others involved in the context also perceive the environment and initiate responses. The responses interact to form an 'enacted environment'. The actors may perceive the environment differently but their perceptual processes and behaviors have contributed to creating it (Smircich and Stubbart, 1985, p. 727; Jablin and Putnam, 2001, p. 201).

One example from our earlier chapter was the entrepreneur who was having difficulties with his marriage and his business. How the entrepreneur perceived his employees and responded to them had combined with their reactions to him to create a situation in which the business was not functioning effectively. The entire set of actors had enacted their environment. The therapist helped the entrepreneur confront the underlying premises on which he was operating. As the entrepreneur changed his behaviors, others began to react differently to him. The entire set of responses contributed to changing the environment in the workplace, which led to greater effectiveness and efficiency in the firm (Kets de Vries, 1996).

When case researchers refer to their work as utilizing an interpretivist approach they signal that they view the phenomenon and its context as a changing social system, complex in nature, and difficult to reduce even to words. Nonetheless they tackle the task of interpreting that phenomenon and its context.

Positivists have a very different perspective. They view the social world as consisting of a reality that is objective and predictable. The world has components that can be measured and subjected to 'scientific' observation and experimental manipulation, the results of which can be tested through statistical analysis tools. To the positivist, the phenomenon under study is reducible to components that can be measured and studied in isolation from other components. The positivists feel strongly that it is necessary to stay separate from the phenomenon in order to retain objectivity about the phenomenon under study. Positivists' research designs tend to be more structured. Their designs involve carefully designed hypotheses and investigatory instruments such as questionnaires or structured interview schedules. They are willing to work with a more limited set of variables with the expectation of an incremental expansion of understanding about the variables under study that relate to the phenomenon and its context.

Given the above descriptions of the interpretivist and positivistic perspectives, it is easy to see why it is often difficult for case researchers and what we will call quantitative researchers to have conversations about the trustworthiness of their findings and indeed about the quality of the research process overall (See Box 6.3 for input into the concept of trustworthiness).[14] Interpretivists use criteria such as credibility, dependability, and

BOX 6.3

ALTERNATIVES TO RELIABILITY AND VALIDITY

Parry (2003) cites Lincoln and Guba (1985) and Guba and Lincoln (1994) in proposing two criteria for assessing qualitative research – trustworthiness and authenticity as alternatives to reliability and validity. Parry was especially interested in trustworthiness because he felt it had more applicability to his own work. He noted trustworthiness are having the four elements which he describes as:

'(1) *Credibility.* Given a constructionist viewpoint that there are multiple accounts of social reality, then the issue in assessing research is not embodied in its "correctness", but in its credibility. This is often based on being seen to follow accepted procedural steps such as grounded theory. Two common techniques to assert credibility are respondent validation (which I used) and triangulation (which I did not). I used respondent validation to ensure I had correctly understood the interviewee's responses and to seek their views on the summary of Weick's theory by Pugh and Hickson (1996). In addition to the problem that respondents may just agree with my interpretation as a means of reinforcing our professional relationship (indeed, no one disagreed with my own categories or Weick's) or may occasion the opposite reaction, that is the censorship of sensitive material, or as Skeggs (1994, p. 86) describes, not actually "understand a bloody word it says", there is an underlying problem with all respondent validation. Mason (1996, p. 151) warns of the dangers of epistemological privilege, the incorrect supposition that an interviewee is in a privileged position to validate the researcher's analysis. Triangulation presupposes that the measurement of a phenomenon from a number of different sources improves the internal validation. This may not be the case and seems to presume there is only one "true" view of the social world which can be "discovered" if triangulation is applied.

(2) *Transferability.* As I have previously said, studying phenomenologically with a small group of executives in my Trust means I must be very careful not to claim that my conclusions could be repeated in other Trusts, or with other executive directors. As Lincoln and Guba (1985, p. 316) describe it, whether findings "hold in some other context, or even in the same context at some other time, is an empirical issue".

One of the ways suggested of increasing transferability or external validation is thick description, but this is not always possible, given the time and space available. I therefore am not concerned on this point as I make no claims of transferability. For the reader who is concerned, my tapes, transcriptions, categories, memos and themes will have to suffice.

(3) *Dependability*. The qualitative equivalent of reliability, this test adopts an audit and transparency approach to field notes, transcripts and so on. However, although Hycener (1985) talks of independent judges I have not read any research that adopts this test (although my

➡

⬅

tapes and notes are available for scrutiny!). As Mason (1996, p. 145) observes, this test is really about the reliability of the research tools, but of course one of those tools is me and I am not neutral or unbiased. Even if you repeated the research, you (or I) may reach different conclusions for a number of reasons involving the researcher, the methodology, and the subjects. This is not to say that issues such as honesty, thoroughness, care and accuracy are not important, but as Mason (1996, p. 146) makes plain, truth and correctness are out of reach to the qualitative researcher.

(4) *Confirmability.* This test is concerned with ensuring the researcher acted in good faith which can only be judged by external audit'.

Source: Parry (2003, p. 256).

---

transferability to judge the quality of their work (Carcary, 2009). To the interpretivist the actors they converse with provide the data that it is the interpretivist's responsibility to interpret and report from that subjective perspective. The interpretivist understands the risk of bias from the influence of their own values. But, the interpretivist relies on 'knowing' by developing an understanding from the perspective of the actors related to the phenomenon and the context within which that phenomenon operates.[15]

In contrast, researchers operating in the positivistic tradition judge their research on the basis of its validity, reliability and generalizability (Carcary, 2009). They often refer to their work as 'empirical' and case research or qualitative research efforts as 'non-empirical', or as one of the authors of this book experienced with the chair of an Institutional Research Board, 'not research at all'. Those operating on positivistic premises are skeptical about the validity of research findings that are not based on objectively measured components of the situation under study.

It is sometimes difficult for the two 'camps' to develop a respectful appreciation for what each brings to helping our social world develop a better understanding of its functioning. The wisest of researchers come to understand the strengths and the limitations of both perspectives. The two perspectives are the 'yin and yang' of our ever-changing challenge of interpreting and interacting with our social world. Some researchers do undertake a combined methods approach. At the University of Kansas where author Taylor was on the faculty for almost two decades, the Strategic Management faculty required doctoral students to initiate their research with a case study. The requirement was put in place because the faculty felt strongly that whatever the phenomenon under investigation, the researcher had to understand the phenomenon from the perspective of those involved in managing it in addition to the perspectives of researchers who had previously studied similar phenomena.

Yin summarized by noting that we need to meet four criteria in order to ensure that the analysis has been done well:

- Has all the evidence been attended to?
- Have all the rival interpretations been addressed?
- Have most of the significant aspects of the study been addressed?
- Has the researcher's prior expert knowledge been used? (Yin, 2009, pp. 160–61)

Yin's wisdom applies whether you are a novice or an expert case researcher. And, his challenge is no trivial one.

6.4   Concluding remarks

In the first section of this chapter we essentially revisited the basic purpose of our research. Are we 'simply' trying to develop a descriptive understanding of the phenomenon under study? Or, are we trying to identify causal relationships among the components of the phenomenon with the anticipation of developing predictive theory and ultimately prescription for practice? These purposes will influence our choice of research design and analysis processes.

In the second section of this chapter we considered the abductive reasoning process, an increasingly widely used process of reasoning. If we are matching to an *a priori* pattern, then we are essentially using a deductive reasoning process. The *a priori* pattern could be a previously developed model or an expected pattern, perhaps based on our personal knowledge of a phenomenon. If there is no expected pattern, then we are essentially using an inductive or grounded theory approach to ascertain what our data may be telling us, or discerning the generalizations that arise from the data itself. Abductive reasoning essentially combines the two by moving back and forth between deductive and inductive reasoning approaches.

The third process, abductive reasoning is admittedly less transparent. However, all researchers, regardless of methodology or reasoning process must ultimately reach that abductive 'Ah ha' stage when they have come to understand the phenomenon.

As you undertake your case research activities, you will undoubtedly undertake an abductive process. As another researcher in the Strategic Management faculty put it, you will come up with an:

> [. . .]inspired guess [because like business practitioners you will find that there is]. . .not enough time or resources to come to complete resolution [therefore]. . .decision-makers have to make their best guess and move to the next stage of problem solving. Abduction helps us to act in the face of ignorance and uncertainty. Our abductions stand in for what we do not or cannot know. They allow us to get on with things (Dew, 2007, pp. 39, 40).

In this sense case research is similar to 'the practice of strategic decision making, rather like detective work [it]. . .is less about "knowing" and more about "guessing"'(Dew, 2007, p. 44). Learning how to guess well – abductive thinking – is core to good designing of good strategy and good research.

Finally, we considered the interpretivist approach to research in comparison to positivistic approaches to research. Those who conduct research with an interpretivist set of assumptions, view the world as a subjective reality. In contrast, a positivist orientation operates with an underlying assumption that the social world can be studied with the same methodologies as the physical world. Positivists take a more detached view of their research subject as imbued with an objective reality that can be measured with precision and subjected to mathematical and statistical techniques. Interpretivists view their role as understanding the phenomenon from the point of view of actors involved in the situation and describing the phenomenon in such a way to be understood by those external to the phenomenon. Case researchers tend to lean toward an interpretivist position. However, your authors point out that both perspectives are important to help us understand our world.

As you move forward in the journey of case research, we trust that you will be willing to embrace the phenomenon you wish to study and take on the both the joy and the challenge of understanding the world through the eyes of your informants. We ask that you remember that they have consented to entrust their lives and experiences with you. Thus, yours is a profound task to help those in your world understand a small slice of it more thoroughly than as if you had not undertaken the case research project or program that is your privilege to pursue.

END OF CHAPTER QUESTIONS AND ANSWERS

1   **How do descriptive, predictive, and prescriptive theory relate to case study research?** A case study research designed to develop descriptive theory describes the context and the state of the unit of analysis at the time of observation. A case study project aimed at descriptive theory will generally have a sample of one. The descriptive theory or model may be the aim of the study or the point of departure for undertaking a more extensive study. A case study project intended to develop a predictive theory states the likelihood of outcome(s) under certain conditions – that is, outcomes are contingent upon identified sets of circumstances as well as the 'error terms' or some as-yet-unidentified circumstances. A case study methodology designed at developing prescriptive theory is intended to provide guidance for the field of practice. It prescribes which actions a practitioner should take because it predicts certain outcome or outcomes likely to occur if the action(s) is(are) taken. Prescriptive theory building follows essentially the same steps as predictive theory building, i.e., data collecting, data categorizing and data analyzing and interpretation of inferred causality.

2   **Why is abductive reasoning important for a case researcher to understand?** The 'Ah ha' experience is shared by researchers regardless of methodology and reasoning principles they follow. The 'Ah ha' occurs when a researcher has come to understand the phenomenon under study. However, the abductive 'Ah ha' is reached through a process that is less transparent than inductive and deductive reasoning processes. Abductive reasoning essentially combines the two by moving back and forth between deductive and inductive reasoning approaches. Abductive reasoning allows the researcher to offer only the best available account of events, not certainty or precise assessment of probability. By identifying overarching patterns that 'connect the dots' of the evidence, the case researcher is essentially a Sherlock Holmes. As Sherlock, the researcher identifies patterns through matching processes and explains critical events through a reasoning process where data generation and data analysis are developed dialectically both sequentially and, sometimes, simultaneously.

3   **What does an interpretivist approach have to do with case study research?** When a case study is undertaken to capture the complexity of phenomena, case study research is linked directly to interpretivist approaches that see the world as messy and complex with multiple realities related to the same phenomenon. The interpretivist's observations of the phenomena are not reducible into measurable components. Thus, the research process calls for an emergent rather than a fixed design. Interpretivist researchers use criteria such as credibility, dependability, and transferability to judge the quality of their work rather than statistical measures of reliability and validity.

NOTES

1   Some researchers are more comfortable with one choice than the others, although the lines between them are often blurred.

2   Klakegg et al. (2010, n.p.) state: 'There are several dilemmas involved in a discussion of how to make an analysis or a system both good and simple at the same time. In Figure 1 [figure omitted], the term "good" is shown as often associated with qualities such as "precise", "objective", "transparent", and "specified". The term "simple" is often associated with qualities such as "easy to understand", "not resource demanding", and "quick and practical". While there is nothing wrong in wanting to have an analysis or system that is both good and simple, the question is whether this is realistic?. . . it is difficult, if not impossible to achieve both'.

3   Thatcher (2006) notes: 'The case study is one of the major research strategies in contemporary social science – or more exactly, in contemporary sociology and political science, as well as social science–oriented professional fields like social work, education, public affairs, and business. What are cases good for? Social scientists have traditionally given two overlapping answers to that question: case studies can

help to identify causal relationships, and case studies can help to understand the worldview of the people they study. The first view, which I will call the "causal case study," has recently been associated mainly with comparative case study research (King, Keohane, and Verba 1994; Ragin 1987), but it also underlies alternative approaches like the extended case method (Burawoy 1998) and the search for mechanisms (Lin 1998; Mohr 1997; George and McKeown 1985). The second view, which I will call the "interpretive case study," is associated with the hermeneutic strand of social science, which aims to illuminate the subjective meaning that people's actions have for them (Geertz 1973). In terminology borrowed from Max Weber, the causal case study contributes to instrumental rationality (*zweckrationalität*) by identifying the consequences actions will have (Weber 1949, p. 26; 1958, p. 151), while the interpretive case study contributes to understanding (*verstehen*) by identifying the motivations and worldview that inform social action (Weber 1978, pp. 7–8).'

4 Note that Professor Bauer received many awards during his time at Harvard Business School. In 1964 he, along with De Sola Pool and Dexter, won the Woodrow Wilson Foundation Book Award for their book, *American Business and Public Policy*. He was also awarded the American Association for Public Opinion Research Award for Exceptionally Distinguished Achievement in 1975 (Raymond A. Bauer Papers, n.d.).

5 Christensen and Carlile (2009) provide the example of man's search for how to fly. The search began during the Middle Ages with observations that most flying beings had wings and feathers. In spite of their many attempts at refining their input variables, the result was often the death of the person who attempted flight. Daniel Bernoulli's study of fluid mechanics in the 1700s (Smid, n.d.) identified the use of an airfoil to produce 'lift' and resulting flight. The implications of the example are that, in order to achieve the outcome of being able to fly safely, one must continue to consider the characteristics of the flight mechanics as well as the situation in order to derive even more explanatory power as well as recommended actions under an identified set of circumstances (Christensen and Carlile, 2009, p. 245). Indeed, the process continues today through a case-by-case analysis of air crashes. The intensive examination of these anomalies provide a stream of additional insights that guide changes in design of the craft as well as behaviors of the pilots in order to achieve the desired outcome of a safely completed flight. As in Bennett's (2004) example, there continue to be mishaps, not only from aircraft design and pilot error, but also from errors emanating from the on-ground personnel in the airport control tower.

6 Grünbaum (2007) argues: 'It is in a nutshell possible to transfer results from just one case to other contexts. Additionally, it is now crystallized what it is the researcher wants to transfer because the case and the unit of analysis are clearly detached' (p. 87).

7 Gerring argues that case study research is distinguished by within-unit variation. Gerring's argument is that research that focuses on only one unit involves a change in the unit – that is, two cases: a before and an after. In short, Gerring argues that in 'trying to intuit a causal relationship from a snapshot – a single case without within-unit covariation – we would be engaging in a truly random operation' (Gerring, 2004, p. 344). He argues that typical case study methodology that involves the study of only one unit involves at least two cases. The multiple cases emanate from the observations about the unit (a) before and (b) after the event or phenomenon under scrutiny. Thus, given Gerring's argument, such a design is two case studies about one site or one subject. The design thus permits observations of the co-variation of the variables or dimensions.

8 There are many case study research projects in which the sample size is one – one subject, as in Professor Kets de Vries's paper (1996), or the case of the Turkish University by Herguner and Reeves (2000). Eisenhardt (1989) opens the door to the possibility of an incremental approach starting with very few cases and augmenting one by one until the incremental insights do not warrant the additional effort.

9 Abductive reasoning was introduced by the philosopher Charles Sanders Peirce (1839–1914). See Anderson (1987).

10 The Allison (1971) study was updated by Allison and Zelikov (1999).

11 The Cuban Missile Crisis began Oct. 22, 1962 when U.S. President John F. Kennedy announced that U.S. spy planes had identified that the Soviet Union had moved missiles on to the island of Cuba, barely 90 miles from the U.S. The 13 days that followed were a tense confrontation that many maintain came very close to war between the two super powers ('October 22, 1962. . .').

12 In garbage-can theory (Cohen, March, and Olsen 1972) an organization 'is a collection of choices looking for problems, issues and feelings looking for decision situations in which they might be aired, solutions

looking for issues to which they might be the answer, and decision makers looking for work' (Cohen et al., 1972, Abstract). Problems, solutions, participants, and choice opportunities flow in and out of a garbage can, and which problems get attached to solutions is largely due to chance.

13 Author Taylor has become more sensitive to this approach while watching especially crime mysteries. For example, the outcome (a murder, a robbery) is known. The detective squad often uses a white board to display data, e.g., pictures of various individuals known or suspected to be associated with the apparent chain of events leading to the crime. The board is likely to include timelines and summaries of facts. The detectives apply the various hypotheses to see if they 'fit' the facts. As they test a particular hypothesis, they may re-review evidence details in more depth or seek additional information. A particular hypothesis may be set aside if the evidence doesn't fit or additional evidence nullifies the hypothesis.

14 The controversy between the "hard" and "soft" sciences has existed for more than a century. Fanelli and Glänzel (2013) note the work of Comte, the 18th Century philosopher who, in the positivistic tradition, proposed a Hierarchy of Sciences from mathematics to sociology. The hierarchy has led to designation of "hard" and "soft" sciences that these two authors note ". . . are used in a vague, confused sense, and their imputation to specific research fields is felt to be controversial if not offensive." (p. 1) See also Wilson (2012); Berezow (2012); 'A different agenda' (2012); and 'Hard and soft science' (2017).

15 However, there are those who clearly disagree that actors in the situation or context can be a useful means of validation of the researcher's observation.

REFERENCES

'A different agenda' (2012), *Nature.* **487** (7407), 271, doi:10.1038/487271a, accessed 31 March, 2017 at http://www.nature.com/nature/journal/v487/n7407/full/487271a.html.

Agar, M. (2010), 'On the ethnographic part of the mix. A multi-genre tale of the field', *Organizational Research Methods*, **13**(2), 286–303.

Allison, G.T. (1971), *Essence of Decision: Explaining the Cuban Missile Crisis*, Boston, MA: Little, Brown and Company.

Allison, G.T. and P. Zelikow (1999), *Essence of Decision: Explaining the Cuban Missile Crisis*, 2nd edition, New York: Addison-Wesley.

Anderson, D.R. (1987), *Creativity and the Philosophy of C.S. Peirce*, Dordrecht: Martinus Nijhoff.

Bauer, R.A., I. de Sola Pool, and L.A. Dexter (1963), *American Business and Public Policy: The Politics of Foreign Trade*, Chicago, IL: Atherton Press.

Bazerman, M.H. (2005), 'Conducting influential research: The need for prescriptive implications', *Academy of Management Review*, **30**(1), 25–31.

BBC News (2012), 'A point of view: The enduring appeal of Sherlock Holmes', *BBC News Magazine*, August 12, accessed 7 March 2017 at http://www.bbc.co.uk/news/magazine-19268563.

Bennett, A. (2004), 'Case study methods: Design, use, and comparative advantages', in F. Sprinz, F. Detlef, and Y. Wolinsky-Nahmias (eds), *Models, Numbers, and Case: Methods for Studying International Relations*, Ann Arbor, MI: University of Michigan Press, pp. 19–55.

Berezow, Alex B. (13 July 2012), 'Why psychology isn't science', *The Los Angeles Times*, np, accessed March 31, 2017 at http://articles.latimes.com/2012/jul/13/news/la-ol-blowback-pscyhology-science-20120713.

Blaikie, N. (1993), 'Research strategies: Retroductive and abductive strategies', in *Approaches to Social Enquiry*, Cambridge, UK: Polity Press, pp. 162–97.

Burawoy, M. (1998). 'The extended case method', *Sociological Theory*, **16**(1), 4–33.

Brown, D. (2003), *The Da Vinci Code*, New York: Doubleday.

Carcary, M. (2009), 'The research audit trial – enhancing trustworthiness in qualitative inquiry', *The Electronic Journal of Business Research Methods*, **7**(1), 11–24.

Carcary, M. (2010), 'Analysing qualitative evidence: The role of CAQDAS', *Proceedings of the 9th European Conference on Research Methodology for Business and Management Studies*, 24–25 June, Madrid, Spain.

Christensen, C.M. and P.R. Carlile (2009), 'Course research: Using the case method to build and teach theory', *Academy of Management Learning and Education*, **8**(2), 240–51.

Cohen, M.D., J.G. March, and J. Olsen (1972), 'A garbage can model of organizational choice', *Administrative Science Quarterly*, **17**(1), 1–25.

Corbin, J.M. and A. Strauss (1990), 'Grounded theory research: Procedures, canons, and evaluative criteria', *Qualitative Sociology*, **13**(1), 3–21.

Dew, N. (2007), 'Abduction: A pre-condition for the intelligent design of strategy', *Journal of Business Strategy*, **28**(4), 38–45.

Doyle, A.C. (1887), *Sherlock Homes, A Study in Scarlet*, London: Ward Lock & Co.

Doyle, A.C. (1890), *Sherlock Homes, The Sign of the Four*, London: Spencer Blackett.

Doyle, A.C. (1902), *Sherlock Homes, The Hound of the Baskervilles*, London: George Newnes.

Eco, U. (1983), *The Name of the Rose*, English edition, New York: Harcourt.

Eisenhardt, K.M. (1989), 'Building theories from case study research', *The Academy of Management Review*, **14**(4), 532–50.

Eshghi, K. (1988), 'Abductive planning with event calculus', in *Proceedings of the 5th International Conference and Symposium on Logic Programming*, University of Washington, Seattle, pp. 562–79.

Fanelli, D. and W. Glänzel (2013), 'Bibliometric evidence for a hierarchy of the sciences', *PLoS One*, **8**(6) doi:http://dx.doi.org.proxy.library.umkc.edu/10.1371/journal.pone.0066938, accessed March 31 2017 at http://search.proquest.com.proxy.library.umkc.edu/docview/1371831065/fulltext/E65924843FFA4C56PQ/1?accountid=14589.

Flick, U. (2006), *An Introduction to Qualitative Research*, 3rd edition, Thousand Oaks, CA: Sage.

Freeman, S., K. Hutchings, and S. Chetty (2012), 'Born-globals and culturally proximate markets', *Management International Review*, **52**(3), 425–60.

Geertz, C. (1973), *The Interpretation of Cultures*, New York: Basic Books.

George, A.L. and T.J. McKeown (1985), 'Case studies and theories of organizational decision making', in R. Coulam and R. Smith (eds), *Advances in Information Processing in Organizations*, Greenwich, CT: JAI Press, pp. 43–68.

Gerring, J. (2004), 'What is a case study and what is it good for?' *The American Political Science Review*, **98**(2), 341–54.

Gold, J., J. Walton, P. Cureton, and L. Anderson (2011), 'Theorising and practitioners in HRD: The role of abductive reasoning', *Journal of European Industrial Training*, **35**(3), 230–46. doi:http://dx.doi.org.proxy.library.umkc.edu/10.1108/03090591111120395; accessed March 10, 2017.

Grünbaum, N.N. (2007), 'Identification of ambiguity in the case study research typology: So what is a unit of analysis?' *Qualitative Market Research*, **10**(1), 78–97.

Guba, E.G. and Y.S. Lincoln (1994), 'Competing paradigms', in *The SAGE Handbook of Qualitative Research*, Thousand Oaks, CA: pp. 105–17.

'Hard and soft science' (2017), *Wikipedia*, March 16, accessed 31 March, 2017 at https://en.wikipedia.org/wiki/Hard_and_soft_science.

Herguner, G. and N.B.R. Reeves (2000), 'Going against the national cultural grain: A longitudinal case study of organizational cultural change in Turkish higher education', *Total Quality Management*, **11**(1), 45–66.

Hycener, R.H. (1985), 'Some guidelines for the phenomenological analysis of interview data', *Human Studies*, **8**(3), 279–303.

Jablin, F.M and L.L. Putnam (eds) (2001), *The New Handbook of Organizational Communication: Advances in Theory, Research and Methods*, Thousand Oaks, CA: Sage.

Kelle, U. (2005), 'Sociological explanations between micro and macro and the integration of qualitative and quantitative methods', *Historical Social Research*, **30**(1), 95–117.

Kets de Vries, M.F.R. (1996), 'The anatomy of the entrepreneur: Clinical observations', *Human Relations*, **49**(7), 853–83.

King, G., R. Keohane, and S. Verba (1994), *Designing Social Inquiry*, Princeton, NJ: Princeton University Press.

Klakegg, O.J., O. Torp, and K. Austeng (2010), 'Good and simple – a dilemma in analytical processes?' *International Journal of Managing Projects in Business*, **3**(3), 402–21.

Kuhn, T. (1962), *The Structure of Scientific Revolutions*, Chicago, IL: University of Chicago Press.

Leavy, B. (2010), 'Design thinking – a new mental model of value innovation', *Strategy & Leadership*, **38**(3), 5–14.

Lin, D (1998), 'An information-theoretic definition of similarity,' *ICML'98 Proceedings of the Fifteenth International Conference on Machine Learning*, pp. 296–304 accessed 31 March, 2017 from http://dl.acm.org/citation.cfm?id=657297.

Lincoln, Y.S. and E.G. Guba (1985), *Naturalistic Inquiry*, Thousand Oaks, CA: Sage.

Mäkelä, T. (2013), Email conversations with Mikael Søndergaard, November 1, 4, 6.

Mason, J. (1996), *Qualitative Researching*, Thousand Oaks, CA: Sage.

McDermid, D. (2006), 'Pragmatism', *Internet Encyclopedia of Philosophy*, accessed 12 March 2017 at http://www.iep.utm.edu/pragmati/.

Millward, H. and A. Lewis (2005), 'Barriers to successful new product development within small manufacturing companies', *Journal of Small Business and Enterprise Development*, **12**(3), 379–94.

Mohr, L. (1997), *The Causes of Human Behavior*, Ann Arbor, MI: University of Michigan Press.

'October 22, 1962: This day in history' (nd), *History*, accessed 31 March 2017 at http://www.history.com/this-day-in-history/cuban-missile-crisis.

Paavola, S. (2004), 'Abduction as a logic and methodology of discovery: The importance of strategies', *Foundations of Science*, **9**(3), 267–83.

Parry, J. (2003), 'Making sense of executive sensemaking: A phenomenological case study with methodological criticism', *Journal of Health Organization and Management*, **17**(4), 240–63.

Peters, T.J. and R.H. Waterman (1982), *In Search of Excellence: Lessons from America's Best-run Companies*, New York: Warner Books.

Peirce, C.S. (1903 [1998]), 'Pragmatism as the logic of abduction (Lecture VII)', in The Peirce Edition Project (ed.), *The Essential Peirce: Selected Philosophical Writings, Vol. 2 (1893–1913)*, Bloomington, IN: Indiana University Press, pp. 226–41.

Porporato, M. (2009), 'Timing and drivers of management control systems in joint ventures: The effect on JV survival', *Qualitative Research in Accounting and Management*, **6**(4), 247–74.

Pugh, D.S. and Hickson, D.J., (1996), *Writers of Organizations*, 5th ed., London: Penguin Books.

Ragin, C.C. (1987), *The Comparative Method*, Berkeley and Los Angeles: University of California Press.

Ragin, C.C. and H.S. Becker (eds) (1992), *What is a Case? Exploring the Foundations of Social Inquiry*, New York: Cambridge University Press.

Raymond A. Bauer Papers (n.d.), 'Bauer, Raymond Augustine, 1916–1977. Raymond A. Bauer Papers, 1941–1980: A finding aid', *Harvard Business School Archives*, accessed 15 September 2013 at http://oasis.lib.harvard.edu/oasis/deliver/~bak00063.

Shah, R., S.M. Goldstein, B.T. Unger, and T.D. Henry (2008), 'Explaining anomalous high performance in a health care supply chain', *Decision Sciences*, **39**(4), 759–89.

Skeggs, B. (1994), 'Situating the production of feminist ethnography', in M. Maynard and J. Purvis (eds), *Researching Women's Lives from a Feminist Perspective*, London: Taylor & Francis.

Smid, T. (n.d.), 'Bernoulli's principle and airplane dynamics: A critical analysis', accessed 12 March 2017 at http://www.physicsmyths.org.uk/bernoulli.htm.

Smircich, L. and C. Stubbart (1985), 'Strategic management in an enacted world', *Academy of Management Review*, **10**(4), 724–36.

Tarr, J.-A. and J. Mack (2013), 'Auditor obligation in an evolving legal landscape', *Accounting, Auditing & Accountability Journal*, **26**(6), 1009–26.

Thatcher, D. (2006), 'The normative case study', *The American Journal of Sociology*, **111**(6), 1631–76.

Van de Ven, A. (1989), 'Nothing is quite so practical as a good theory', *Academy of Management Review*, **14**(4), 486–9.

Visconti, L.M. (2010), 'Ethnographic case study (ECS): Abductive modeling of ethnography and improving the relevance in business marketing research', *Industrial Marketing Management*, **39**(1), 25–39.

Weber, M. (1949), *On the Methodology of the Social Sciences*, Glencoe, IL: The Free Press of Glencoe. (Translated and edited by Edward A. Schils and Henry A. Finch; accessible at http://fs2.american.edu/dfagel/www/Class%20Readings/Weber/weber_on_methodology_of_social_sciences.pdf).

Weber, M. (1958), 'Science as vocation', in H.H. Gerth and C. Wright Mills (eds), *From Max Weber*, New York: Oxford University Press, pp. 129–56.

Weber, M. (1978), *Economy and Society*, Berkeley, CA: University of California Press.

Weick, K.E. (1995), *Sensemaking in Organisations*, Thousand Oaks, CA: Sage.

Weick, K.E. (2001), *Making Sense of the Organization*, Oxford: Blackwell.

Wilson, Timothy D. (12 July 2012). 'Stop bullying the 'soft' sciences: The social sciences are just that – sciences', *The Los Angeles Times*, accessed 31 March 2017 at http://articles.latimes.com/2012/jul/12/opinion/la-oe-wilson-social-sciences-20120712.

Yin, R.K. (2009), *Case Study Research: Design and Methods*, 4th edition, Thousand Oaks, CA: Sage.

7

Wrapping it up and 18 capsules of 'what you need to remember most'

In Chapters 2 through 6 we introduced you to a great deal of material aimed at helping you with your case research journey. What we want to do here is to simply recap in 18 capsules the major items we believe you need to remember most.

7.1 The 18 capsules

1. Know why *you* are undertaking this journey. The more you put into it, the more you will get out. However, we must be realistic as each of us is limited by time and other resources. Be realistic as you undertake this initial step of self-analysis. Your results will affect the choices you make for every other aspect of your case research journey.
2. Establish an objective for the research.
3. From the objective, design the research questions. The questions may be preliminary and subject to change. But start with at least one or more.
4. Be clear about the unit of analysis you are going to study. And, remember always that as a case researcher, you are studying the unit of analysis *within* its context.
5. Think carefully about whether you are going to study one unit or multiple and whether you are going to study the unit/s at a point in time or longitudinally.
6. Read and understand the literature that relates to the phenomenon you are studying.
7. Descriptive, predictive, and prescriptive theory matter – establish which you are aiming for.
8. Understand the pros and cons of qualitative and quantitative data.
9. Establish whether you will aim to gather primary or secondary data or both.

10. Understand that garnering primary data will require not only site selection, but also finding avenues to enter the site or sites, maintaining relationships with gatekeepers, and exiting gracefully.

11. Be aware of the special considerations related to data gathering when you use interviewing, participant observation, and internal and external documentation as your sources of data.

12. Think carefully about the use of content analysis as applied to your data and whether you need to take the time to learn to use QDAs.

13. Use Professor Yin's advice for data analysis if it is appropriate to do so.

14. Consider abductive reasoning as the approach to understanding your data.

15. Weigh the possibility of using an interpretivist mode in developing an understanding of the research data.

16. Remember! Patience, persistence, and politeness contribute to good management of site entry, engagement, and exit. They also help when dealing with the analysis phase of the research.

17. Reliability and validity are important in case research. Thus, keeping an 'audit trail' of the process and having your work reviewed by both those involved in the case situation and colleagues knowledgeable about such phenomena are important.

18. Take a little time to watch the great detective, Sherlock Holmes – no doubt he will offer some additional clues about cases, data, and analysis.

7.2 Summing it up

The issues we have pursued above must be put in the context of the totality of the roadmap we have presented in this book. In Chapter 1, Figures 1.1 and 1.2 summarize the issues as you undertake one, or multiple, case studies in order to develop a better understanding of some slice of the world we live in.

As suggested in Chapter 2, be sure to understand yourself and why you are undertaking this particular research, what the objective or end goal of your research is, and what unit of analysis you are going to focus on.

Chapter 3 reminded us that there are many research designs to choose from. In case research, basic research designs involve the number of cases and whether the data we gather will help us understand our subjects at a point in time, or over an extended period of time.

Chapter 4 provided insights into managing research sites, data and information sources challenges. In executing our research we must address very practical issues such as identification of, entry into, and, ultimately, withdrawal from our research sites. We will have to think about the specific data that we want to obtain and what the specific information sources are that may yield that data. Once we begin to acquire data or information about the subject we are studying we need to explicitly consider the manner in which we will analyze that information. Yin (2009), whose work spans several decades, has had a powerful influence on approaches to case research design and data analysis. Yin's recommendations can help make especially multiple-case design projects more manageable in the analysis phase.

In Chapter 5 we focused on some of the dilemmas of undertaking analyses of our data. However, as Chapter 6 suggests, we must remember that analyses are undertaken only when we understand the theoretical contributions we are trying to make, the differences among inductive, deductive and abductive reasoning and, finally, where we personally position ourselves in the interpretivist-positivistic continuum of assumptions and premises.

Our research can help us learn about a portion of the world we live in and to provide reflection for ourselves and our audience on what that world is like (descriptive), how it works under certain conditions (predictive) and, finally, what we might do to help our world function more effectively (prescriptive). Our task as researchers is a privileged role of being, at least temporarily, set aside as the reflective learning facilitators for our world.

Your roles as a student and a researcher often have an uneasy alliance – the process of moving from one to the other is not always easy. If you are an undergraduate student, you are typically learning what others have learned and transmitted through written or spoken media. As a researcher you are drawing knowledge from the phenomenon itself and reconfiguring that knowledge to generate new knowledge to be transmitted. Franken (2012), who worked extensively with international students from Asia undertaking graduate research studies in a New Zealand program referred to this process as re-situation. She describes re-situation as involving:

> [. . .]understanding of the new situation, recognizing what knowledge and skills are needed in the situation, extracting them from the context(s) of previous learning, transforming them to fit the new situation, and integrating them with other knowledge and skills in order to think/act/communicate in a new situation (Franken, 2012, p. 847, with reference to Eraut, 2004, p. 256).

We must understand that this shift in roles from learner to researcher is no trivial challenge.

In this final and concluding chapter we have revisited this book through 18 capsules of what we believe you need to remember most. We believe they will be useful to you as you undertake your case research journey.

Finally, thank you for sharing this journey with us. As we developed this book, we learned a great deal from revisiting our own and our students' research experiences as well delving into those of other researchers. We hope you learned even half as much from reading this material!

Let us know how your case research journey goes – we would be delighted to have some fresh examples for the revision of this book.

REFERENCES

Eraut, M. (2004), 'Informal learning in the workplace', *Studies in Continuing Education*, **26**(2), 247–74.

Franken, M. (2012), 'Re-situation challenges for international students "becoming" researchers', *Higher Education*, **64**(6), 845–59.

Yin, R.K. (2009), *Case Study Research: Design and Methods*, 4th edition, Thousand Oaks, CA: Sage.

Index